CHART SENSE
for WRITING

Over 70 Common Sense Charts with Tips and Strategies to Teach 3-8 Writing

Rozlyn Linder, Ph.D.

The Literacy Initiative

Atlanta

Chart Sense for Writing: Over 70 Common Sense Charts with Tips and Strategies to Teach 3-8 Writing

www.ChartSense.RozLinder.com

CHART SENSE is a trademark of The Literacy Initiative, LLC.

541 Tenth Street Suite 258, Atlanta, Georgia 30318

Cover and Interior Design: Buzz Branding, LLC.

Library of Congress Cataloging-in-Publication Data

CIP data is on file with the Library of Congress.

ISBN: 978-0-9889505-2-8

Printed in the U. S. A.

This book is dedicated to Brandy McDonald, Sarah Klein, Kelli Sowerbrower, and Erika Cooper. You guys are what educators should be. Each of you is a ROCKSTAR and I strive to be as smart, talented, and humble as each of you.

Acknowledgements

I want to thank all of the teachers across the nation who have let me come into their classrooms, train them, and learn from them! This book could not have been possible without the support of so many people. Often the people who inspire you the most get the least amount of thanks.

While I travel to schools in many different states, I first began working with Georgia teachers. I want to thank the teachers, staff members, and principals at Eastside Elementary, Annette Winn Elementary, and Chestnut Log Middle School in Georgia. Almost two years ago, you were my first group of educators to embrace explicit writing instruction and modeled writing. Your dedication to writing instruction and to your students is amazing and often goes unsung. Thank you for being an inspiration!

While there are so many teachers that I am eternally grateful for, a few will stay with me forever: Kelli Rowsey, Tiffany McBean, Zarinaha Satterwhite, Tisha Weaver, Andrea Battle, and Sabrina Britt. You ladies are awesome, encouraging, and rocked out writing in a way that I could only dream of!!! Watching you teach students to build strong paragraphs, develop details, and assess their own writing was inspiring and telling. Kelli, thank you for letting me come to your class and get the superstar treatment from your students. Britt and Tisha, thanks for taking a small nugget from me, remixing it, and making it work for all learners. Z—thanks for teaching me some serious lessons about how to run a writing class, motivate students, and demand excellence from students. Watching you teach is inspiration on its own! Tiffany (always flawless) thanks for reminding me that, as teachers, we are more than just what we do day-to-day in the classroom. Andrea, thank you for both letting me spend time with your students and motivating me with words of encouragement, kindness, and support. Finally, back to Britt. Thanks for your X-Men story, breaking the rules, and keeping kids first. You kept us laughing when it seemed like the road ahead was long and arduous. Your early encouragement, our Olive Garden runs, lots of laughter, and hard work contributed to this labor of love in more ways than you know! Thanks so VERY MUCH!!!

SECTION TWO: Production and Distribution of Writing

Standard 4: Organization & Style — 103

Standard 5: Revision & Editing — 119

Standard 6: Technology & Writing — 139

SECTION THREE: Research to Build and Present Knowledge

*C*hart Sense for Writing is designed as a resource to help you create effective charts that support the writing standards. The first section, *Why Charts?* explains why charts make a difference in classrooms. There is also a detailed list and explanation of the materials that you need to create and display effective charts.

Each subsequent chapter is devoted to a different writing standard. The chapters are labeled to match the exact standard that they represent. For example, chapter one is all about writing standard one; chapter two is all about writing standard two, and so on. This allows you to easily turn directly to the standard that you need.

Once you turn to the chapter that you need, the very first page of the chapter lists the Common Core anchor standard. Anchor standards are the broad, overarching standards that apply to all grade levels. Underneath the anchor standard are the writing standards broken down by grade level. You can easily find your grade level, highlight your standard, and review the specific language of that standard. The standards are worded exactly as they are on the Common Core State Standards Initiative website, sponsored by the National Governors Association Center for Best Practices (NGA Center) and the Council of Chief State School Officers (CCSSO). You can access this directly at: http://www.corestandards.org.

The writing standards vary vastly from the reading standards. There are four types of writing represented in the standards. These include the first three genre-driven standards: argument/opinion, informative/explanatory, and narrative writing. Hidden way down on the list, as standard nine, is another genre that doesn't get much attention as a writing standard. This is the literary analysis standard. This type of writing focuses on analyzing text. The remaining standards simply support these four core writing types. Standards four through eight don't exist in isolation; they are standards that support the development of the other writing genres. Finally, just as with reading, standard ten is not included in this book. This, to me, is a teacher standard that is embedded and taught throughout the year through the other standards.

As you move through the chapters, each additional page features a different instructional chart specific to that writing standard. Detailed notes are provided to explain how the chart can help grow writers, how to create your own chart, and any grade-level specifications for that chart.

While there are many different charts included here, the idea is not for you to create each chart! The goal is to give you some ideas to support instruction. These charts can be duplicated exactly as they are pictured here or varied and adapted for your classroom. If you adapt a chart or create an even more dynamic version, tell me about it! I am always excited to see and hear what new ideas and creative instructional decisions teachers make. Questions? Need help? Reach out to me online at www.rozlinder.com. Happy teaching!

Dr. Roz

At-a-Glance

The *Chart Sense for Writing* table of contents is organized by the Common Core writing standards. While this is a helpful framework to sort the charts, sometimes, as a writing teacher, you are looking to introduce a writing skill simply because you know that your writers need it. This At-a-Glance section highlights some of the most common writing skills and a few of my favorite charts to help with these key skills.

Writing Skill(s)	Charts
Adjectives and Adverbs	*Ways to Build a Two-Adjective Sentence, page 72* *Adjectives Can Compare, page 80* *Develop Settings and Characters, page 84* *Look for Adverbs and Adjectives, page 86*
Citing Textual Evidence	*Citing Textual Evidence, page 42* *How to End an Argument, page 44* *Incorporating Evidence, page 46* *Researchers Paraphrase, Cite and Synthesize, page 176*
Creating Leads/ Hooks	*Reasons to Begin with Multiple Questions, page 50* *Ways to Begin an Informative Text, page 70* *Types of Hooks, page 96* *Three-Part Leads, page 110*

Writing Skill(s)	Charts
Developing Topic Sentences	This is Hard (or Easy!), page 54
	Crafting Topic Sentences, page 62
Elaboration	Building Mighty Paragraphs, page 58
	Writing About Historical Events, page 74
	Writing About People, page 76
	Elaboration Ideas, page 122
	Writers Share Anecdotes, page 136
	Animal Research, page 154
Transitional Words	Six Types of Transitions, page 52
	Transitions Help Your Writing, page 94
	Don't Be a Bore, page 108
Varying Sentence Structure	Rename Your Subject, page 124
	Say NO! to Lonely Subjects, page 130
	Vary Your Sentences, page 134
Writing Conclusions	How to End an Argument, page 44
	Narrative Endings, page 88

Why Charts?

When I first wrote *Chart Sense: Common Sense Charts for Teaching 3-8 Informational Text and Literature*, I wanted to show teachers how to use charts to engage students and make reading skills more accessible. Since the publication of the Chart Sense series, I have been able to visit classrooms across the nation and see the different ways that charts are used to impact student learning. I am more convinced than ever of the powerful role that charts play in making learning visible, not just for reading, but for writing as well. Whether you teach using the Common Core writing standards, state standards, or locally-developed standards, students still need more support than ever to write about literature, craft narratives, and build informative/explanatory and argument text. Shared visuals are an easy and effective way to help support students in *any* subject area. I find that students have a stronger sense of ownership over the content, use the charts as learning tools more often, and are more engaged and interested.

1. Students will have a shared sense of ownership over the content.

You are creating these charts with your students. This is not a situation where you tell them to do something and hope that they do it. This is something that you create with your students through discussion, questioning, and a shared sense of learning. You will notice that students revel in having their writing on a chart or recognizing the sections that they contributed to. When a shared writing chart falls off the wall, your students will actually rush to pick it up and get it back into place. These shared creations will belong to the entire class.

2. Students will use the charts!

You can easily visit your favorite school supply store to stock up on lots of charts to decorate the walls of your classroom. Those charts may be attractive, but do they really impact instruction? How many times have you seen a student use one of those commercial charts? Five? Ten? Make one chart with your students, and watch how many more times they use that chart!

3. Visuals are engaging!

Charts give students a visual reminder of what is expected, how to get there, and ways to troubleshoot. Often, students may not ask for help or admit that they don't remember a strategy. Having a consistent visual reminder is an appealing way to trigger their memories and to keep their attention. Think about the typical fashion magazine. Some of these magazines are 50% advertisements! From a financial standpoint that infuriates me, but I still catch myself gazing at the attractive spreads to see what they are selling. My curiosity is piqued, and I actually keep the image in my head. Creating an attractive visual with your students is just one way to tap into that same phenomenon, but for writing skills.

Different Types of Charts

There are many different types of charts. They can be organized and classified in a dozen (or more) different ways by a dozen (or more) different experts. I like to think about charts as reminders for students. They help students to keep track of their learning and to apply it. Relying on this belief, I classify charts into four key areas:

1. Ritual

2. Toolbox

3. Classification

4. Interactive

Ritual

These types of traditional charts can be found in virtually every K-12 classroom. Ritual charts usually display the basic rules that students should follow. These can include behavior, classroom expectations, or arrival/dismissal procedures. Many of the procedural charts that teachers make for writer's workshop typically fall into this category as well. Ritual charts are introduced at the beginning of the year or unit, and they rarely change. These charts, while important, are very specific to your own classroom. They will vary based on the norms, beliefs, and programs adopted by your school and district. As a result, *Chart Sense for Writing* does not include this type of chart.

Toolbox

Toolbox charts remind me of a day, not too long ago, when I watched a car mechanic pulling out his red, weathered toolbox to try to diagnose my car. The tattered toolbox seemed to be filled with everything he needed. I watched with curiosity as he lifted my hood, then proceeded to pull out a wide variety of tools. I found myself questioning and wondering what exactly was going on. What was that black thing? Why does he have two of those? What is that pointy thing? Why did he put that tool back in the box?

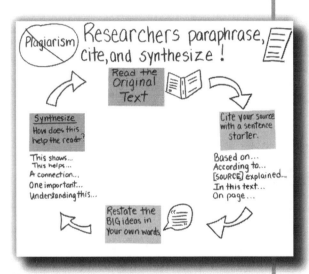

Toolbox chart example

Students can rely on a toolbox of strategies to plan, draft, revise, and publish their writing. Toolbox charts represent that collection of strategies. Students certainly aren't fixing a car with these tools, but they are just as powerful. Toolbox charts help students to understand options for what to do when they struggle, get confused, or need help determining what to do next. These types of charts could include steps to follow when working on a specific standard or problem-solving strategies. Toolbox charts are introduced throughout the year. They can help you introduce a unit of study or serve as activators. These charts are also created in response to student performance. If I notice that most of my writers are coming to a roadblock when they try to revise effectively, I may develop a chart that helps them understand the concrete steps that they can follow to assess how and when to begin revision. This might take the form of a list or a sequence of steps. I often add additional information and grow these charts throughout the year as students develop new writing skills and tools.

Classification

Classification charts can be used when your students need to understand unique or different characteristics. For example, genre charts that list the features of argument, explanatory, or narrative writing would fit into this category. Classification charts are also useful when students need to compare and contrast genres. Teachers can use these types of charts to help students keep track of big ideas and categorize information. Students can use these charts as visuals to help them organize their research as well.

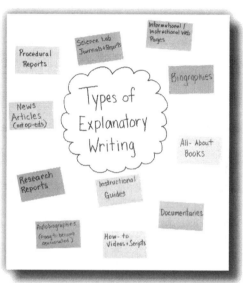

Classification chart example

These charts can include lists, webs, or other graphics. Classification charts can also be used to develop initial understanding or to redirect a misunderstanding. These can be introduced at any time throughout the year.

Interactive

Interactive charts are my absolute favorite. I find that students learn the most from these types of charts. Interactive charts can be static or reusable. Students generate the information, and it is specific to a particular type of writing. For example, if I teach my students to vary their sentence structures, we would also create a chart to go along with it. This chart would be a short paragraph that we could write as a class. This collaborative process results in meaningful charts that differ from year to year. Not only are these charts created with the students, but they also include an active think-aloud modeling session.

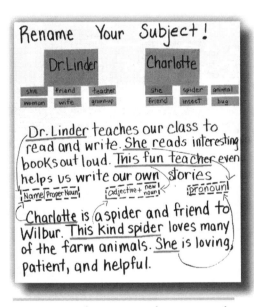

Interactive chart example

Think-aloud modeling means that as you write, you stop to question, wonder, and let students have a peek into your cognitive process. Interactive charts usually remain in a prominent place, and they serve as exemplars. Sticky notes work hand-in-hand with this type of chart. For example, as students organize their writing, they can use sticky notes to record the type of details, examples, or sentence types that they rely on. Interactive charts are great spaces to share and post these ideas. The sticky notes can also be removed or repositioned depending on the type of writing that the class is crafting.

Please keep in mind that each of these different chart categories are not rigid boxes that must remain separate. There will be overlap, and some charts could belong in more than one category. The category is not the most important thing here; the teaching is.

Materials to Create Great Charts

It is not necessary to be an artist or to spend tons of money to create effective charts for your writers. There are some basic tools that you will want to have on hand to make charts easily.

Chart Paper

There are many different brands and styles of chart paper. There are types that have adhesive on the back and can be stuck right onto the wall. These work well, but they will eventually lose their adhesive quality and possibly fall down. This process will happen even faster if you move your charts around a lot. The easy solution is to add tape. But… if I have to add tape, then I might as well use regular chart paper, right? Well, there are pros and cons to all types of chart paper. Let's take a look:

Paper Type	Benefits	Disadvantages
Adhesive-Back Chart Paper	You can quickly attach these to any wall in seconds. These are readily available in most office supply stores.	These may eventually fall down without the addition of more tape. This is the most expensive choice.
Non-Adhesive Chart Paper	Most school and office supply stores carry this paper. This is the most inexpensive choice.	You must use tape or magnets to display this type of chart.
Half-Sized Chart Paper	These are great for quick charts that don't require a full-size sheet.	You may still need to purchase full-size paper for larger charts.
Non-Adhesive Colored Chart Paper	These bright charts are the most attractive of all the options.	A limited number of stores carry this paper. This is more expensive than plain white chart paper.

Chart paper comes in a variety of sizes and colors. One of the largest sizes of chart paper is 25"x30". This size chart comes in yellow or white. You can choose lined, blank, or grid-lined for the surfaces. This size chart paper is used for most of the charts in this book. If you are interested in colored chart paper, Pacon® sells spiral bound chart paper that is about this same size (24"x32") and comes in assorted pastel colors. For brighter colors, consider Top Notch Teacher Products' 24"x32" neon chart paper. Also spiral bound, these tablets contain eye-catching deep oranges, greens, pinks, and blues. The second largest size, 20"x23", is commonly associated with easel pads. This size comes unlined, with primary lines, and blank. Finally, there are small, colored paper chart tablets that are about half the size of the larger size chart paper. At 24"x16", these charts take up less space and work well for charts that contain small amounts of information.

Sticky Notes

Sticky notes are essential when creating reusable charts. They can easily be filled out in advance and repositioned as necessary. In order to maximize this flexibility, I try to keep a wide variety on hand.

Post-it® brand notes are readily available in many shapes, sizes, and colors. One of my favorites is the large 8"x6" size. This size sticky note is used a lot for the large headings and for many of the interactive charts. The small 4"x4" sticky notes are very common, but often too small for younger students to

Sticky notes come in a wide variety of sizes and colors.

write on. They run out of room quickly. Reserve these for your own text. 6"x4" sticky notes are larger and work well when you need students to write information for charts. Both of these sizes tend to cost more, but they really help your charts stand out and provide more space to write on.

A cheaper alternative to emulate the effect of the oversized sticky note is to grab a pack of colored paper and tape. You can cut the paper into any shape or size, then use a small amount of tape to stick the note onto your chart.

While I tend to stock up on the large sticky notes, sometimes you need a tiny strip or a very small sticky note. These can be used to mark a section or add words during guided revision. The smallest size Post-it® brand sticky notes that I recently started using for these purposes are the ½"x2" size and the 1"x3" size. Post-it® calls these *page markers*. These tiny notes are great when adding a list of words in a small space.

Organize Your Narrative!
1. Select a story type. CvC CvH L+F CvN
2. Identify the BIG Challenge.
3. Create at least ONE Setback. STOP
4. Resolve/Fix the challenge OR Decide that the challenge is okay as is.

The small sticky notes here are Post-it® page markers.

Thin-Tip Markers

I like to have thin, student-friendly markers on hand. Many brands categorize these types of markers as fine-tip or fine-point markers. These markers work best for your students to use when they need to write on the charts or add information. These thin markers also come in handy when you need to illustrate something more elaborate, write on a page marker, or draw a simple detail. Crayola®, Rose Art®, and Sharpie® all sell great thin-tip markers. I have even found several office supply store brands to work just as well.

Wide-Tip Markers

I use wide-tip markers most frequently when writing on charts. I have tried many different brands, shapes, and sizes. This choice really comes down to personal preference. For a long time, I relied only on the scented Mr. Sketch® markers. In the past few years I have also discovered the wide-tip Sharpie® brand markers. Both brands are excellent choices for making charts. Be careful to avoid any markers that are labeled as "poster markers." These tend to be much too big for charts, and they also bleed through chart paper.

Sentence Strips

Sentence strips are long pieces of sturdy paper, resembling cardstock. One side has a guideline rule, while the other has a single line. You can find sentence strips in white, beige, rainbow, and pastel colors at school supply stores and big-box retailers. They only cost a few dollars and one pack goes a long way.

In the nineties, when I first started creating charts with my students, I never even thought about adding sentence strips to a chart. Why would I do that? Couldn't I just write the same information on the actual chart or on a sticky note? Eventually, I found that sentence strips were surprisingly useful when making charts. They are larger than most sticky notes and much more durable. They also come in handy when students need to record more than just a few words on a chart. There are times when you will need to add long sentences, write descriptive phrases, or even quote lengthy passages of text. Sentence strips can provide the extra space necessary to do this.

Scissors

You want to keep a pair of reliable scissors on hand. There will be times when you will need them to cut your sticky notes and sentence strips into various shapes and sizes. Consider using craft scissors with different types of edges to add a decorative effect. These come in zig-zag, scallop, ripple, and curved shapes. Typically sold in sets of six or twelve, these scissors are available at most craft stores and big box retailers. Popular brands include Fiskars® and X-Acto®. Make sure that you have a few extra pairs on hand for student use as well.

Adhesive

Masking tape is a useful resource to keep on hand. You will need this to hold charts up and attach paper to the charts. I prefer this type of tape because it can easily be removed when you need to reposition different elements of your chart. If you are a fan of clear or double-sided tape, be certain that what you are taping down does not need to be manipulated by your students often. The last thing you want to do is rip a hole in one of your charts.

Space for Charts

Every classroom is arranged differently, and school districts have varied rules about how wall space can be used. Optimally, you will have lots of blank walls and the ability to put as much (or as little) on the walls as you choose. In reality, this is rarely the case. It is usually necessary to explore alternative options for displaying your charts. If your students cannot see the charts, they can't use them. Here are some of the ways I display my charts.

The Clothesline

I first started using the clothesline method when I was a fourth-grade teacher. I bought an actual clothesline at a big-box retailer, two nails, and plastic clothespins. I asked our wonderful custodian if he would place the two nails in opposite corners of my room. We hung a clothesline that spanned the length of my classroom. I learned a few valuable lessons that year. When you hang such a long clothesline diagonally, only half of the class can see any particular chart at the same time. I also learned that chart paper doesn't like to stay attached to a clothesline without reinforcement. One chart actually took four or five plastic clothespins to stay in place. Also, this meant that our entire class was always drowning under a sea of charts.

The next year I reworked my whole clothesline idea. I had to admit that I'd grown overly attached to my charts, and just wanted my handiwork visible at all times! That was the wrong approach; I had to let it go. This time I hung the clothesline flat against one wall. I learned that I did not need every chart hanging up at the same time. Only charts that students are actively using need to be displayed in a classroom.

Magnets

One simple way to display your charts is to hang them on a chalkboard or a whiteboard using magnets. Two or three magnets will easily hold up most charts. The use of magnets gives you the flexibility to post and remove your charts as needed. This also allows metal file cabinets or any other metal surfaces in your classroom to become display areas.

Hangers

Skirt or pants hangers work well to display charts. You should be able to inexpensively pick up a few at the local dollar store. When buying clothing from any retailer, ask the cashier if you can keep your hangers. You can even ask for some of the extra hangers that are almost always in a big box under the cash register. I have walked out of stores with over thirty pants hangers. It doesn't hurt to ask!

A chart hung from a pants hanger

Once you have your hangers, you can use them to easily hang any non-laminated charts. Laminated charts tend to be slippery and will slide out of the clips. You can store your charts by hanging them out of the way on doors or cabinets until you need them. You can also use a garment stand to hold the hangers. I like this idea because your students can go over and access any chart that they need, even after you retire it from the wall. If you live close to an IKEA, consider purchasing a *Rigga* or a *Mulig* clothing stand. Both stands cost around ten dollars apiece and can even be ordered online at www.ikea.com.

Hidden Gems

Don't overlook the obvious. A chart can be displayed in many different places. If you have fabric curtains covering a bookcase, grab two safety pins and attach your chart to the front of the curtain. Depending on how your room is organized, the marker or chalk holder at the base of your chalkboard or whiteboard is a perfect space to hang several charts. Do you have large classroom cabinets? The doors and sides of those cabinets could be great landing spots for charts. Check out your classroom windows, the front of your desk, the bottom of a mounted television, or even the extra space above your chalkboard. Think about places that normally go untouched. Be creative and look for hidden gems!

Chart Ideas: Alternatives from Fellow Teachers

On a flight to New York, I met a teacher who was a fan of creating charts with her students. She shared some of the creative ways that she relied on to display and use charts with her students. Despite her inventiveness, she just had too many charts around her room. She felt that she was swimming in paper! I have found that this happens to teachers more often than not!

Since writing the original *Chart Sense,* I have heard feedback from teachers about how they create and teach with charts. I always hear great ideas. Some of the most interesting ideas are those that relate to alternative methods to store, display, or access charts. Check out some of these methods from fellow teachers across the nation:

Chart Binders

Consider creating your writing charts, then snapping pictures after you have introduced and used them with your students. Store the chart pictures in sheet protectors to create your own chart binder. Some teachers organize the charts with dividers numbered by the standard or writing genre. This binder can easily become a resource for upcoming school years, serving as a visual reminder of what worked (or did not work) the previous year. Some teachers even create binders and place them in a central location for students to access. Add a table of contents and you have a class set of resources ready to go.

Student Sets

Another great idea is to let students create some of the charts at their desks alongside you. The logic here is that students not only interact and receive instruction when you build the larger chart, but that they all have the same experience of developing and recording the chart information. This works as a form of note-taking and encourages students to create and organize their own writing resources. Some teachers distribute three-pronged folders and ask students to keep a record of the different writing strategies and charts. I have seen these called *Strategy Folders, Writing Tools,* and *Skill Journals.*

Go Digital

In classrooms with whiteboards, teachers can rely on these as storage tools for the charts. A team of fifth-grade teachers shared that they never use actual chart paper to create their charts. Instead, they draw them on their whiteboards, save them, and print them out. Students get the actual drawing, and the saved chart is accessible for later revision or extension.

Smaller Charts

Another way to avoid becoming inundated with charts is to go small! Instead of full-size charts, some teachers cut the chart paper in half. This allows for more charts to be visible at once, but take up half the space.

Teachers who use this strategy talk about the ease of creating these half-size charts. They also find it easier to group and display charts throughout the room, and for students to manipulate and access the charts.

PowerPoint® Archive

In other classrooms where students have reliable access to computers, teachers use PowerPoint® slides to create charts. You can take a picture of your chart and insert it into the slide, or you can insert a saved image from your whiteboard. Both are easy to do. I watched one teacher create a chart on her regular dry-erase board, snap a picture with her phone, email it to herself, and within two minutes she had pulled it up and dropped it into a PowerPoint® slide labeled with the writing skill. This file grew throughout the year and become an archive of writing strategies. The PowerPoint® was always accessible for students. When they began to work, I noticed students open the slide show and click until they reached what they were looking for. Other teachers have saved their PowerPoint® file on a shared drive or network that is accessible from home or school. Parents and students alike can access any of the charts developed in class.

Chapter 1

Arguments & Opinions

Common Core Writing Anchor Standard 1:

Write arguments to support claims in an analysis of substantive topics or texts, using valid reasoning and relevant and sufficient evidence.

3

Write opinion pieces on topics or texts, supporting a point of view with reasons.
a.   Introduce the topic or text they are writing about, state an opinion, and create an organizational structure that lists reasons.
b.   Provide reasons that support the opinion.
c.   Use linking words and phrases (e.g., because, therefore, since, for example) to connect opinion and reasons.
d.   Provide a concluding statement or section.

4

Write opinion pieces on topics or texts, supporting a point of view with reasons and information.
a.   Introduce a topic or text clearly, state an opinion, and create an organizational structure in which related ideas are grouped to support the writer's purpose.
b.   Provide reasons that are supported by facts and details.
c.   Link opinion and reasons using words and phrases (e.g., for instance, in order to, in addition).
d.   Provide a concluding statement or section related to the opinion presented.

5

Write opinion pieces on topics or texts, supporting a point of view with reasons and information.
a.   Introduce a topic or text clearly, state an opinion, and create an organizational structure in which ideas are logically grouped to support the writer's purpose.
b.   Provide logically ordered reasons that are supported by facts and details.
c.   Link opinion and reasons using words, phrases, and clauses (e.g., consequently, specifically).
d.   Provide a concluding statement or section related to the opinion presented.

6

Write arguments to support claims with clear reasons and relevant evidence.
a.   Introduce claim(s) and organize the reasons and evidence clearly.
b.   Support claim(s) with clear reasons and relevant evidence, using credible sources and demonstrating an understanding of the topic or text.
c.   Use words, phrases, and clauses to clarify the relationships among claim(s) and reasons.
d.   Establish and maintain a formal style.
e.   Provide a concluding statement or section that follows from the argument presented.

7

Write arguments to support claims with clear reasons and relevant evidence.
a.   Introduce claim(s), acknowledge alternate or opposing claims, and organize the reasons and evidence logically.
b.   Support claim(s) with logical reasoning and relevant evidence, using accurate, credible sources and demonstrating an understanding of the topic or text.
c.   Use words, phrases, and clauses to create cohesion and clarify the relationships among claim(s), reasons, and evidence.
d.   Establish and maintain a formal style.
e.   Provide a concluding statement or section that follows from and supports the argument presented.

8

Write arguments to support claims with clear reasons and relevant evidence.
a.   Introduce claim(s), acknowledge and distinguish the claim(s) from alternate or opposing claims, and organize the reasons and evidence logically.
b.   Support claim(s) with logical reasoning and relevant evidence, using accurate, credible sources and demonstrating an understanding of the topic or text.
c.   Use words, phrases, and clauses to create cohesion and clarify the relationships among claim(s), counterclaims, reasons, and evidence.
d.   Establish and maintain a formal style.
e.   Provide a concluding statement or section that follows from and supports the argument presented.

Types of Opinion Writing

This introductory chart is a way to transition from informative or narrative writing into opinion writing. Created with fourth graders, this chart is best suited to the lower grades. If you decide to create this with older students, simply change the center from *opinion* to *argument.*

Creating This Chart:

1. Decide how many different types of opinion writing you want to share with your students. For third and fourth graders you may want to only include five or six. The ones that I would omit when working with younger students include *literary analyses, debate notes,* and *persuasive essays.* Remember that my list is not definitive and should be adjusted based on your local curriculum and classroom needs.

2. Gather digital or print examples of each. If you cannot locate a good exemplar, craft your own to share with students.

3. As you add the sticky note for each type, share an example with students, but really focus on *why* the example represents opinion writing.

Variations:

- Ask students to help come up with categories to add to the chart. Even if their examples are incorrect, this still opens up a lively discussion about why some types of text are not examples of opinions.

- Consider adding *movie reviews* as a category. This is always fun, and there are lots of exemplars for this type of opinion writing.

- Student opinion and argument writing (unedited) can be found here: http://achievethecore.org/content/upload/ArgumentOpinion_K-12WS.pdf.

- Op-eds can be found here: http://learning.blogs.nytimes.com.

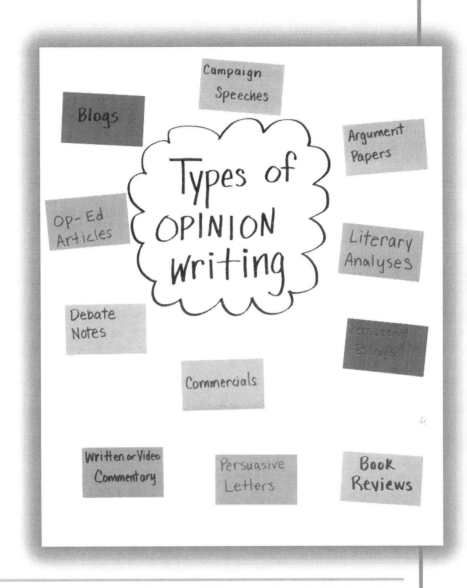

Figure 1.1 *Types of Opinion Writing* chart

Acknowledge a Counterclaim

This chart was created with sixth graders. They were working on argument essays that had at least two distinct sides. When we made this chart, students had already planned their essays and were beginning to draft their introductions.

Introducing This Chart:

I write the title on the chart and ask students what they think a *counterclaim* is. We spend a few minutes discussing the term. We end with the notion that a counterclaim is the opposite side of the issue that the author is writing about. Then, I add each sticky note and discuss the sentence starters. I ask students to discuss which one they like best and why. Students generally begin to talk about why different sentence starters are "better" than the others. This can lead to discussions of tone, audience, formality, and purpose.

Counterclaims in Opinion and Argument Writing:

There are multiple and varied opinions about the shift from opinion writing to argument writing after fifth grade. Many people see these as drastically different types of writing, while others treat them as synonymous terms. I tend to fall in the middle. Many of the same teaching points exist for both types.

When I teach arguments, I require that students acknowledge counterclaims. Acknowledging the counterclaim is not exclusive to argument writing; students who are writing opinions can include counterclaims to build a stronger paper as well. Note that this chart is simply about acknowledging a counterclaim. You may ask students to acknowledge the counterclaim and offer their own claim, or to elaborate and refute the counterclaim.

Acknowledge a Counterclaim

One viewpoint is...

Many people think... support... argue... Claim...

On one hand ...

There is some support for the idea that ...

Granted, some might argue... support... believe...

It could be argued that ...

Figure 1.2 *Acknowledge a Counterclaim* chart

Argument Bookmark

This chart was created when working with eighth graders. Students were preparing to take a state exam and needed to respond to an isolated writing prompt. Many of the students had great points to support their claims, but lacked organization and elaboration.

Why a Bookmark?

After instruction, I type up a version of this chart and print copies out as bookmarks for each student. Some teachers laminate the bookmarks or wrap them with clear packing tape to make them more durable for students. Others have taped them on desks or inside writing folders. The goal is for students to use the bookmarks frequently so that they begin to automatically remember how to organize their arguments.

Writing Patterns:

This bookmark is a definite pattern for writing. I find that most students need a pattern. Without an organizational structure, many don't know where to begin. The great part about introducing a pattern is that once students have a general understanding of an effective way to organize their writing, they can begin to vary the pattern and individualize it.

Breaking This into Smaller Chunks:

1. Create this chart one section at a time. Consider only discussing paragraph one on the first day. Ask students to take an older topic (or assign one) and practice the development of just that paragraph. Build up more each day before applying these skills to an independent topic.

2. Create charts to provide sentence starters for the different components. For ending thoughts, see the chart *How to End an Argument* on page 44. For charts on explaining evidence, see *Incorporating Evidence* on page 46 or *Citing Textual Evidence* on page 42. For a chart on types of details, see *Argument Tactics* on page 38. For suggestions on explaining different points, see *Building Strong Argument Body Paragraphs* on page 40.

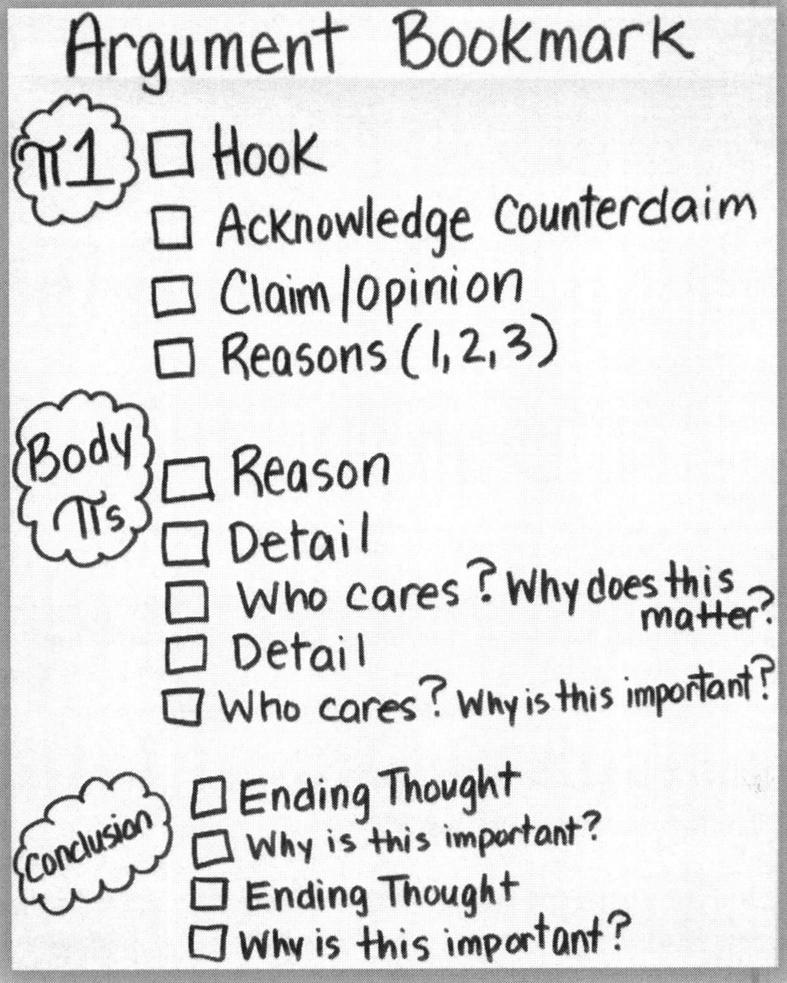

Argument Bookmark

¶1
- ☐ Hook
- ☐ Acknowledge Counterclaim
- ☐ Claim/opinion
- ☐ Reasons (1, 2, 3)

Body ¶'s
- ☐ Reason
- ☐ Detail
- ☐ Who cares? Why does this matter?
- ☐ Detail
- ☐ Who cares? Why is this important?

Conclusion
- ☐ Ending Thought
- ☐ Why is this important?
- ☐ Ending Thought
- ☐ Why is this important?

Figure 1.3 *Argument Bookmark* chart

Argument Tactics

This chart was created with eighth graders. The chart serves as a reminder of the different types of ideas that students can use to elaborate within their body paragraphs.

Creating This Chart:

1. Select four or five tactics that you want your students to begin using in their essays. Discuss each one and add it to the chart. Avoid adding more than that at one time.

2. When you add a tactic, be sure to discuss the benefits and drawbacks of each. For example, when I add *Emotional Appeals,* we talk about how this could be useful to appeal to a reader's emotions, but could also be overdone and make an argument look weak or without valid logical support.

Understanding the Tactics:

Each tactic is simply an approach for supporting claims or refuting counterclaims. For example, *Slippery Slope* tactics try to explain how one action or event will slowly lead to a series of other undesirable events. This is different from *Causation* because it implies that the shifts are gradual and typically only negative. Most of the ideas listed here are pretty straightforward, but a few can be confusing. This section explains some of the more nuanced tactics listed here:

- *Alternatives* is a tactic where the author is not renouncing a counterclaim, but simply showing that there are better choices that exist.

- *Precedent* is showing where a similar event has been debated and that the resolution or correct response is again warranted with the author's current argument.

- *Analogies* is the practice of comparing the claim to something else (a different topic/subject) and pointing out a relationship or drawing a comparison to make a point.

- *Flawed Logic* is when the author focuses on the mistakes in the counterclaim. This is not about developing a claim, but rather about poking holes in the reasoning behind a counterclaim or general viewpoint.

Figure 1.4 *Argument Tactics* chart

Argument Body Paragraphs
Building Strong

This chart was created with seventh graders, but is really effective with elementary school students as well. I find that we spend a lot of time in writing classrooms teaching about beginnings and endings, but limited time helping students sort out how to develop the meat of their essays: the body.

Introducing This Chart:

1. I draw the title and illustration on the chart and ask students, *"What makes a paragraph strong?"*

2. After hearing different ideas, I lead students to the conclusion that strong body paragraphs have three parts.

3. Then, I write each checkbox on the chart, explaining each one.

4. On the board, or on a blank chart, I write my own paragraph. As I write the paragraph, I switch colors for each of the three parts, thinking out loud to reinforce how I am following the checklist to develop my body paragraph.

Student Practice:

After modeling, I ask students to chose between two authors or books. For this group, I asked them to choose between Walt Whitman and Emily Dickinson. Students had recently read poems by each. Students were to write one paragraph arguing which author was best. For each new point that a student argued, they repeated this sequence. The next day, students shared their paragraphs. We spent about a week just focusing on developing strong body paragraphs with different topics and points. This was powerful and fun for students. The next week, students began to work on arguments, incorporating this learning into crafting larger essays.

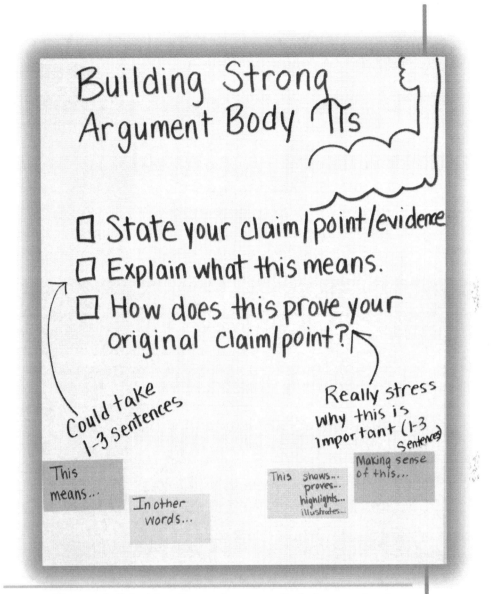

Building Strong Argument Body ¶s

☐ State your claim/point/evidence

☐ Explain what this means.

☐ How does this prove your original claim/point?

Could take 1-3 sentences

Really stress why this is important (1-3 sentences)

This means...

In other words...

This shows... proves... highlights... illustrates...

Making sense of this...

Figure 1.5 *Building Strong Argument Body Paragraphs* chart

Citing Textual Evidence

This chart was created with a group of third graders. A variation of this chart, *Incorporating Evidence* (page 46), was also created with seventh graders. Both serve the same purpose. Draw from each to get ideas for helping students to reference evidence in their writing. You have probably seen dozens of evidence sentence starters. The difference with this chart is that students are not just referencing the evidence, but they are explaining the context. Telling why the evidence matters is critical. This shifts the use of textual evidence away from listing and closer to synthesis.

Introducing This Chart:

1. Before writing anything on the chart, I begin with an open-ended question. I ask students, *"If you saw something really interesting on television last night and wanted to tell me about it, how might you start your sentence?"*

2. If I don't get any responses, I probe students by giving examples. *"If I heard something serious on the news, I might come in the next day and say that CNN said that…"*

3. I continue giving examples until students start sharing ideas that fit under the *What does your source say?* side.

4. After a brief discussion, I begin adding the sentence starters to the chart.

5. Next, I ask for volunteers to tell me how to begin a sentence to share evidence from a source. Then, I ask students to select a second sentence to help me understand why this matters. *"Why should I care?"*

6. A quick and easy way to practice this strategy is to watch commercials with the class. Then, ask students to write one sentence to share what the commercial (source) says and a second sentence to show why this information matters. This is always fun and helps the learning to stick.

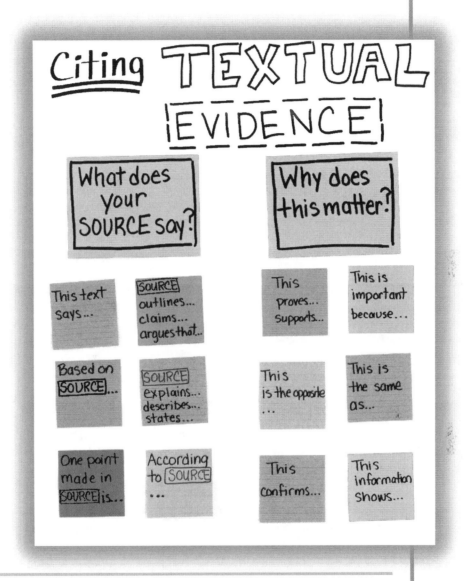

Figure 1.6 *Citing Textual Evidence* chart

How to End an Argument

Students are often taught to write conclusions by restating the original thesis or claim, listing the three main points, and rewording the thesis again. I hate to admit it, but that is how I was taught to write a conclusion as well. The confusing part about this method is that it isn't actually how real arguments end. Think about it. If you read a news or opinion article supporting a particular political candidate, it does not end by saying, "*Joe Politician is not a good mayor. First, … Second … Lastly, …Mr. Politician is a bad choice.*" That would be the worst! So why do we keep telling kids to do this?

Introducing This Chart:

1. I begin by telling students how dry conclusions are that follow that old, redundant formula. *"They are so boring!"*

2. Next, I explain that there are some ways that students can break that pattern and try something new.

3. I write each of the four ways to end an argument on the chart and draw a box around each one.

4. Afterwards, I share sentence starters for each one, encouraging students to verbally complete the starters with mock topics.

5. After we try out several different sentence starters, I ask students to choose two of the ending thoughts from the chart for their own essays. To build a more substantial conclusion, students then add a sentence explaining the relevance of each ending thought. We call this pattern: *Ending Thought-Who Cares?-Ending Thought-Who Cares?* This seems silly, but it reminds students to elaborate on each of the ending thoughts that they include in their essays. This adds length and clarity.

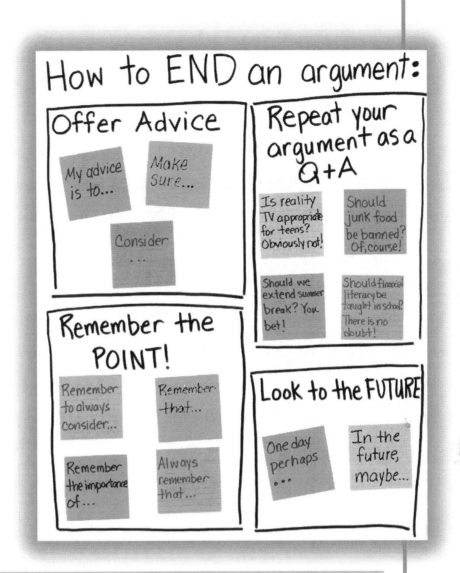

Figure 1.7 *How to End an Argument* chart

Incorporating Evidence

Textual Evidence. You hear this all of the time. Students are supposed to recognize it, write about it, and talk about it. When it comes to incorporating it into their writing, students suddenly start to plagiarize, or they produce a long list of random information from a book or other source. This chart is my solution to that.

Teaching With This Chart:

1. I begin by telling my students that we are going to take a break from writing today and watch a few commercials.

2. I show students one commercial. A great site for commercials is http://www.superbowl-commercials.org/. Be sure to preview in advance.

3. At this point, I add the six sticky notes on the *source says…* side. I don't add the title or anything yet. Next, I ask students what the commercial was about. "*What do you think the company behind the commercial wants us to learn or remember?*" The only rule is that they have to begin their sentences with one of the sentence starters.

4. After several students have shared, I add the six sticky notes on the right side of the chart. I repeat one of the sentences that students have just shared with me, but add a second sentence using one of the new sentence starters from the right side of the chart. I call on volunteers to do the same.

5. We watch several other commercials and repeat the process.

6. After students seem to get the hang of it, I add the title and the other parts of the chart. I explain that they already know how to incorporate evidence by using these two steps.

7. In subsequent lessons, I refer back to the commercials and emulate this same process with textual evidence.

Incorporating Evidence

source says...	why does this matter?
According to...	This shows...
This text details...	This proves...
The author states... asserts... suggests...	This is important because...
Based on...	This helps...
This article describes...	This challenges...
[SOURCE] explains...	This supports...

say it! + explain it!

Figure 1.8 *Incorporating Evidence* chart

Plan Like an Alien

This chart was born from the need to write on demand. Time was limited, and my fifth graders needed a way to plan on the fly and move into a first draft in record time. This odd-looking creature is basically a planning web, with a quick twist.

Creating This Chart:

1. I draw the circle, two legs and a lone antenna in the middle. I have students do the same thing at their desks. I intentionally keep the conversation light and fun. *"That looks crazy, right guys? Well sometimes when you have to write in a bit of a hurry, you have to do some crazy things!"*

2. Then, I throw out a silly opinion topic. For this chart, it was cats vs. dogs. Use something that is simple and fun for your students. I have used sports, entertainers, movies, genres, etc.

3. I ask students to outline the two sides by writing a basic topic sentence for each one on both sides of the antenna.

4. Now that students have both sides clearly named, I ask them to be the judge and put the winning side in the middle. Which side will they write about? For this chart, I had students tell me some of their topic sentences. I put some of these responses on my chart. Students only write their own sentence down.

5. I point out how skinny the legs are. To make them strong enough to hold up this giant body, the reasons need to be solid. This is where we write two reasons to support the opinion written in the center of the body.

6. At this point, I have students look at what they've written. They have a topic sentence, two reasons, and a sentence that acknowledges the counterclaim. These are the bones of an introductory paragraph and the topic sentences for two body paragraphs.

7. Why two body paragraphs? Why not three? For elementary students, I prefer two strong body paragraphs instead of three. I have rarely seen a student name three strong supporting ideas. Two are usually solid, followed by a variation of the other or a weak third one. I'd rather focus on adding great details and elaboration to develop two strong body paragraphs.

Figure 1.9 *Plan Like an Alien* chart

Reasons to Begin with
Multiple Questions

Students are constantly reminded to craft interesting introductions. In an effort to engage the reader, students try out different strategies. One of the most misused strategies that I encounter is the rhetorical question; I have seen students use this strategy in all types of ineffective ways. While more skilled writers can use this appropriately, it is a challenge for most students, particularly reluctant or younger writers. To help students be more effective when they use questions, we created this chart.

Teaching With This Chart:

1. I asked the class to name ways to hook a reader. Almost immediately, the suggestion to ask a question or multiple questions came up. I explained that writing a question does not automatically make your beginning engaging. There had to be a *purpose* behind that question. *"What is the point of the question? If there is no reason for it, choose a different strategy!"*

2. One reason to begin with a question could be to indicate the author's stance. For example, I might write: *Is it fair to take away the rights of women? Definitely not.* The purpose of asking and answering this question is to let the reader know the author's viewpoint. We called this the Q & A strategy. This was easy to understand; we did not need a chart to clarify this part.

3. Next, we talked about when a writer would use multiple unanswered questions. I told students that there were four reasons when multiple questions made sense. I drew the first box and wrote *evoke emotion* inside of it. I explained that this is one reason to use multiple questions at the beginning of an essay. Next, I wrote an example in the box.

4. I continued this process with the other three reasons, followed by examples. Afterwards, I asked students to look at an older draft that they had written and test out one of these types of multiple questions. Finally, I had them share with a partner to discuss which beginning was more effective.

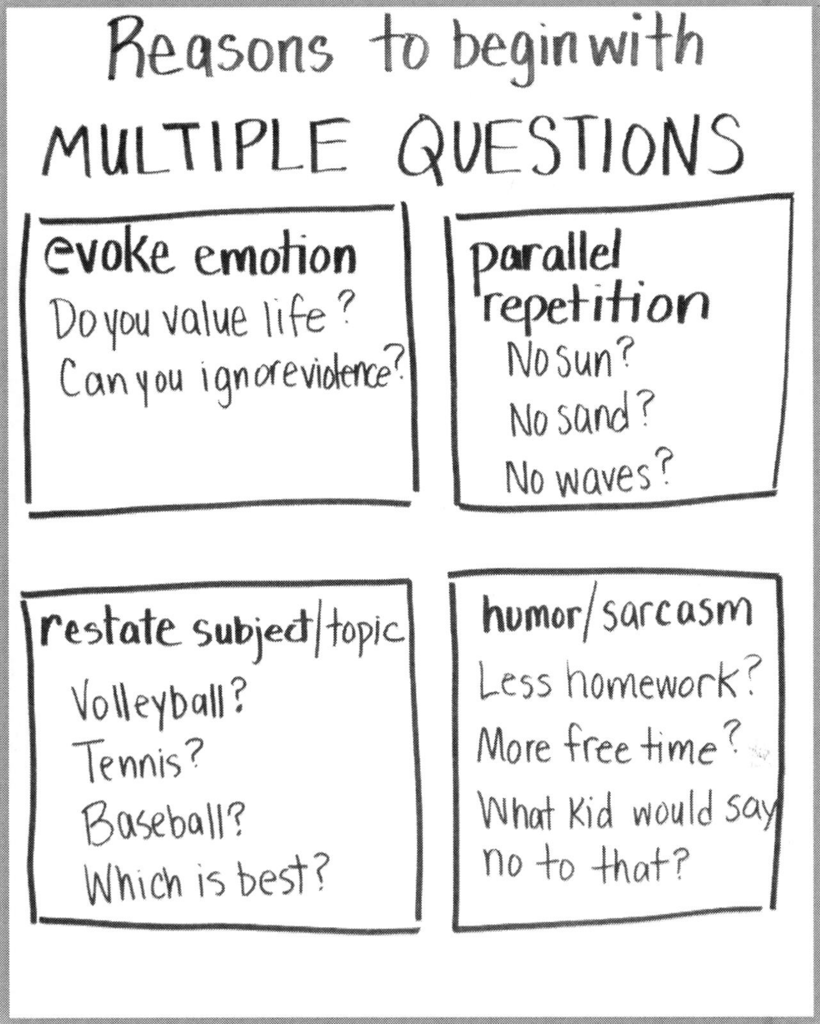

Reasons to begin with MULTIPLE QUESTIONS

evoke emotion
Do you value life?
Can you ignore violence?

parallel repetition
No sun?
No sand?
No waves?

restate subject/topic
Volleyball?
Tennis?
Baseball?
Which is best?

humor/sarcasm
Less homework?
More free time?
What kid would say no to that?

Figure 1.10 *Reasons to Begin With Multiple Questions* chart

Six Types of Transitions

Students are regularly taught that writers use transitions to move to different ideas within a piece of writing. Unfortunately, many students think that sequence words, followed by commas, are the only types of transitions that exist. This often results in a very limited use of transitions and an overuse of sequential transitions. Students of all ages can benefit from a chart like this one to expand and vary their use of transitions.

Creating This Chart:

I create this chart from start to finish with students. I simply ask them to divide a sheet of paper into six boxes. While I name each type of transition, I have students replicate my larger chart and simultaneously create their own charts in their notebooks. We move through each one and add examples. Notice that *finally* has an asterisk beside it. That simply indicates that this word could serve multiple transitional purposes. My list here is not definitive. Modify it, as needed, to fit your needs.

Variations:

- Write each one of these on large sticky notes. Use the wall or another flat surface to build this chart without the chart paper.

- Gather digital or print text that uses these transitions to share with your students as exemplars.

- Pair students in teams or groups, then challenge them to find paragraphs that include these types of transitions.

- Add one or two types of transitions at a time. Build up the list over the course of your unit.

- This chart can be useful with other genres as well. For example, the *Time Passing* category works particularly well with narrative writing.

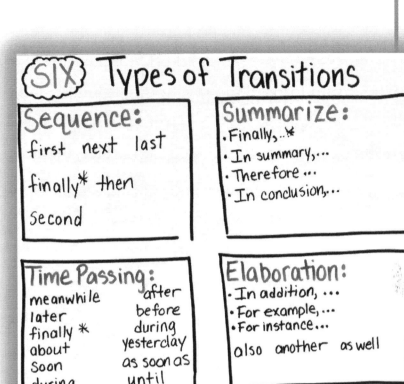

SIX Types of Transitions

Sequence:
first   next   last
finally*   then
second

Summarize:
• Finally,...*
• In summary,...
• Therefore...
• In conclusion,...

Time Passing:
meanwhile   after
later   before
finally *   during
about   yesterday
soon   as soon as
during   until

Elaboration:
• In addition, ...
• For example,...
• For instance...
also   another   as well

To Compare:
• In the same way,...
• Similarly,...
• Likewise,...
like   also   as   just like

To Contrast:
• On the other hand,...
• Although...
• Even though...
but   yet   otherwise
still   despite

Figure 1.11 *Six Types of Transitions* chart

This is Hard (or Easy!)

This is a great chart to help stretch out introductions. Typically, students create thesis statements that name their points in just one sentence. When students do this, they end up with nothing much left to write in their introduction. We encourage them to provide context, background, or hook their readers in this space. While these are all viable options, the introduction can still seem too short. One way to tackle this is to have students begin with a *this is hard* or *this is easy* statement. This type of sentence works well with argument writing because it either acknowledges the complexity of a topic, or implies that there is only one obvious stance (situating the counterclaim as implausible).

Creating This Chart:

1. I begin by discussing topics that the majority of my students would choose similar sides for. For example, *"Should the driving age be moved to 21?"* Anything regarding rights for students or personal freedom typically works well.

2. After I share topics, I ask, *"Was that a difficult choice? Was it an easy choice?"*

3. Then, I ask about more nuanced topics. Topics like: which classes should be offered, extending the school day, or deciding who is the smartest person in the building typically work well. I ask if these topics are as simple to decide.

4. Once students come to the conclusion that some decisions are easy to make, while others are more complicated, I tell them that this is a great way to start an argument essay. *"Let your reader know the weight of your topic from the start. This builds up your topic and gives you a bit of length without giving away your points at the first sentence."*

5. Finally, I add the sentence starters and endings to the chart. I call on volunteers to practice writing sentences using the different words.

This is hard (or easy)!

Making the choice...	complex
Deciding...	difficult
The debate about...	nuanced
Choosing between...	complicated
	challenging
The discussion about...	hard
Determining...	almost impossible
	daunting
Making a decision...	clear
Explaining... **	simple
Describing... **	clear cut
Detailing... **	obvious
	multi faceted

Figure 1.12 *This is Hard (or Easy!)* chart

Chapter 2

Informative/Explanatory Text

Common Core Writing Anchor Standard 2:

Write informative/explanatory texts to examine and convey complex ideas and information clearly and accurately through the effective selection, organization, and analysis of content.

3

Write informative/explanatory texts to examine a topic and convey ideas and information clearly.

a. Introduce a topic and group related information together; include illustrations when useful to aiding comprehension.
b. Develop the topic with facts, definitions, and details.
c. Use linking words and phrases (e.g., also, another, and, more, but) to connect ideas within categories of information.
d. Provide a concluding statement or section.

4

Write informative/explanatory texts to examine a topic and convey ideas and information clearly.

a. Introduce a topic clearly and group related information in paragraphs and sections; include formatting (e.g., headings), illustrations, and multimedia when useful to aiding comprehension.
b. Develop the topic with facts, definitions, concrete details, quotations, or other information and examples related to the topic.
c. Link ideas within categories of information using words and phrases (e.g., another, for example, also, because).
d. Use precise language and domain-specific vocabulary to inform about or explain the topic.
e. Provide a concluding statement or section related to the information or explanation presented.

5

Write informative/explanatory texts to examine a topic and convey ideas and information clearly.

a. Introduce a topic clearly, provide a general observation and focus, and group related information logically; include formatting (e.g., headings), illustrations, and multimedia when useful to aiding comprehension.
b. Develop the topic with facts, definitions, concrete details, quotations, or other information and examples related to the topic.
c. Link ideas within and across categories of information using words, phrases, and clauses (e.g., in contrast, especially).
d. Use precise language and domain-specific vocabulary to inform about or explain the topic.
e. Provide a concluding statement or section related to the information or explanation presented.

6

Write informative/explanatory texts to examine a topic and convey ideas, concepts, and information through the selection, organization, and analysis of relevant content.

a. Introduce a topic; organize ideas, concepts, and information, using strategies such as definition, classification, comparison/contrast, and cause/effect; include formatting (e.g., headings), graphics (e.g., charts, tables), and multimedia when useful to aiding comprehension.
b. Develop the topic with relevant facts, definitions, concrete details, quotations, or other information and examples.
c. Use appropriate transitions to clarify the relationships among ideas and concepts.
d. Use precise language and domain-specific vocabulary to inform about or explain the topic.
e. Establish and maintain a formal style.
f. Provide a concluding statement or section that follows from the information or explanation presented.

7

Write informative/explanatory texts to examine a topic and convey ideas, concepts, and information through the selection, organization, and analysis of relevant content.

a. Introduce a topic clearly, previewing what is to follow; organize ideas, concepts, and information, using strategies such as definition, classification, comparison/contrast, and cause/effect; include formatting (e.g., headings), graphics (e.g., charts, tables), and multimedia when useful to aiding comprehension.
b. Develop the topic with relevant facts, definitions, concrete details, quotations, or other information and examples.
c. Use appropriate transitions to create cohesion and clarify the relationships among ideas and concepts.
d. Use precise language and domain-specific vocabulary to inform about or explain the topic.
e. Establish and maintain a formal style.
f. Provide a concluding statement or section that follows from and supports the information or explanation presented.

8

Write informative/explanatory texts to examine a topic and convey ideas, concepts, and information through the selection, organization, and analysis of relevant content.

a. Introduce a topic clearly, previewing what is to follow; organize ideas, concepts, and information into broader categories; include formatting (e.g., headings), graphics (e.g., charts, tables), and multimedia when useful to aiding comprehension.
b. Develop the topic with relevant, well-chosen facts, definitions, concrete details, quotations, or other information and examples.
c. Use appropriate and varied transitions to create cohesion and clarify the relationships among ideas and concepts.
d. Use precise language and domain-specific vocabulary to inform about or explain the topic.
e. Establish and maintain a formal style.
f. Provide a concluding statement or section that follows from and supports the information or explanation presented.

Building Mighty Paragraphs

Students are not just responsible for writing full essays. Students have to respond to open-ended prompts and develop constructed responses across multiple content areas. This chart, created with sixth graders, is a guide for that type of writing.

Introducing This Chart:

1. I begin by telling students that we are going to work on open-ended paragraphs. I describe these as responses where you ditch the introductory and conclusion paragraphs, and get right to the best, juiciest, body paragraph.

2. I specify that I expect at least two main points in any constructed-response/open-ended paragraph. These are identified as *facts* on the chart. We called them this because we were working on explanatory writing. To use with argument or opinion writing, change to *point, claim,* or *reason.* Some teachers like to use *point* because they find that it works interchangeably with each genre.

3. I create the list and explain each one. For the final section, number 8, I explain that this is the section where you summarize, synthesize, or put everything in context. *"What is the takeaway for the reader?"* I draw parallels between this step and conclusion paragraphs in longer pieces.

4. To include additional facts or points, simply duplicate steps 2, 3, and 4. Regardless of the number of points, students always end with the *who cares?* sentence.

Teaching Ideas:

1. Type up a version of this list and give one to each student. Ask students to check or initial that they have completed each step before submitting their work.

2. After students have worked with this chart for a while, challenge students to create new steps, move steps, or expand steps. You will be surprised at how creative students can be with this type of request.

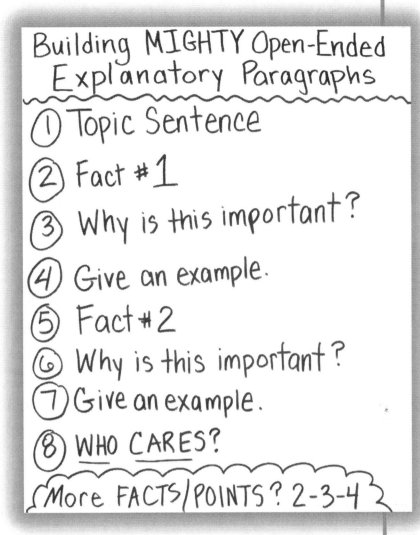

Figure 2.1 *Building Mighty Paragraphs* chart

Compare/Contrast Informative Writing

Informative/explanatory writing can be organized in lots of different ways. This chart, completed with seventh graders, offers a step-by-step guide for organizing a compare/contrast paper.

Introducing This Chart:

- This straightforward chart is written from start to finish with students. I simply list each step and spend a few moments talking about each one. The steps themselves are typically not new or confusing for most students. The real new learning is the pattern of organization.

- I tell students that this chart is a roadmap that provides a clear pattern that we are going to try out when drafting comparison essays.

Variations:

- Just like some of the other charts, this is a great chart to transform into a bookmark or checklist. Simply type each line with a checkbox next to it instead of a round bullet. You can fit 2-4 checklists on a standard-size piece of paper. To save paper, you could also have students write down each step to make their own checklists. When students submit their work, they can check off each element that is included within the body of their essays.

- Use this format when writing a pro/con paper or any type of writing that analyzes the advantages and disadvantages of a topic.

- Instead of creating the entire chart, reveal a few steps at a time, guiding students through their essays. After the guided essays, students can complete their own independent comparison essays on different topics, using the first set of essays as exemplars. Remember to modify each of these steps to meet the needs of your students. This pattern is just one way to organize this type of writing.

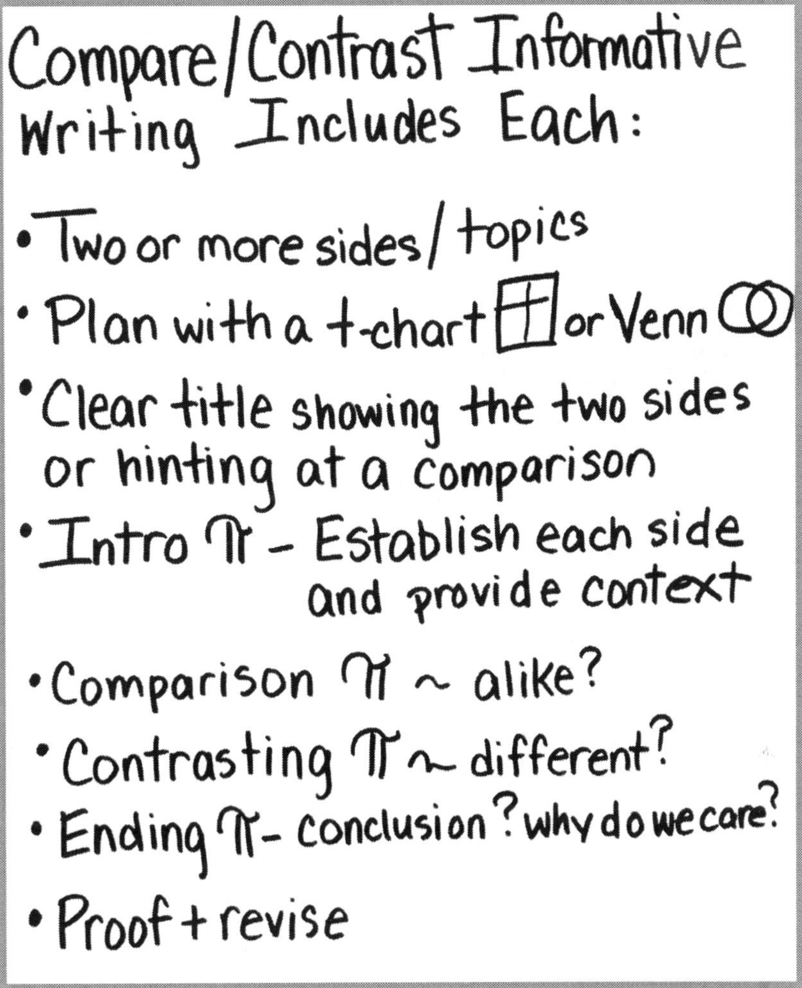

Compare/Contrast Informative Writing Includes Each:

- Two or more sides / topics
- Plan with a t-chart ⊞ or Venn ◌◌
- Clear title showing the two sides or hinting at a comparison
- Intro ¶ – Establish each side and provide context
- Comparison ¶ ~ alike?
- Contrasting ¶ ~ different?
- Ending ¶ – conclusion? why do we care?
- Proof + revise

Figure 2.2 *Compare/Contrast Informative Writing* chart

Crafting Topic Sentences

This chart is versatile. I have created this chart to help students develop a topic sentence for body paragraphs and to develop the first sentence in response to shorter, open-ended prompts in an effort to craft constructed responses. This example was created with eighth graders who were preparing to take a test where they had to read two different texts and then write about them. Students did not know what type of prompt they would receive; they only knew that it would require some type of explanation and connection between the two texts.

Crafting Topic Sentences:

1. I add the title, divide the two sides, and write the headings.

2. On the left side of the chart I add sticky notes that reflect four possible purposes for writing. On the right side, I add two different sentence starters for each type of writing, and we discuss each one.

3. Then, I read a prompt out loud. After I read the prompt, students use the sentence starters to write topic sentences for that prompt. Students know that they are not actually writing full responses to any of these prompts; they are just using these examples to test drive this strategy.

4. After each one, students discuss their topic sentences in small groups. Then, we reconvene and each group shares at least one example. Afterwards, I read a new prompt, and we repeat the process.

My Prompts:

I use prompts that the students are already familiar with from books or from other subject areas. I need students to be familiar with the topics, but they do not need extensive knowledge for this activity. My prompts for this day are:

- *Explain the similarities and differences between the Union and Confederate soldiers.*
- *Describe the contributions of Madame C.J. Walker.*
- *Describe the pros and cons of Westward expansion.*
- *Explain the causes of the Civil War.*

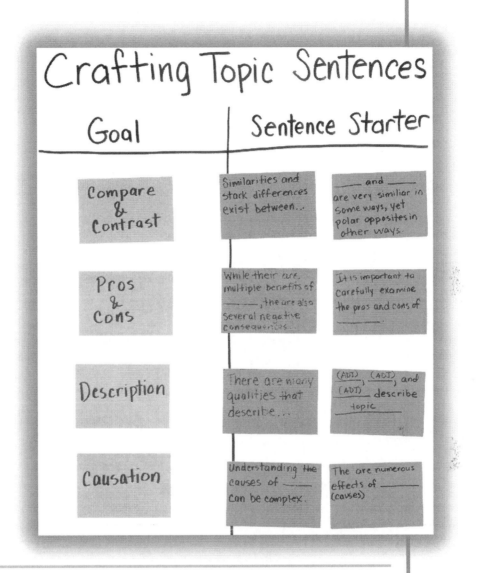

Crafting Topic Sentences

Goal	Sentence Starter
Compare & Contrast	Similarities and stark differences exist between... / _____ and _____ are very similar in some ways, yet polar opposites in other ways.
Pros & Cons	While their are multiple benefits of _____, the are also several negative consequences... / It is important to carefully examine the pros and cons of _____.
Description	There are many qualities that describe... / (ADJ), (ADJ), and (ADJ) describe topic.
Causation	Understanding the causes of _____ can be complex. / The are numerous effects of _____ (causes)

Figure 2.3 *Crafting Topic Sentences* chart

Grouping Explanatory Writing

This chart, created with sixth graders, serves multiple purposes. It can easily be used when talking with students about crafting explanatory or argument writing. This chart is also a great blend of the learning from standards two and four.

Creating This Chart:

1. I begin by writing the title and labeling each side.

2. I tell students that we can think about explanatory/informative writing in two ways. Sometimes we want to present two sides of an issue. This is represented on the left side.

3. The right side represents when we need to write about steps or characteristics. This type of writing requires us to organize information into groups.

4. I add the names of different types of writing on sticky notes. I read each one and ask students to talk with a partner about which type of organization is involved with each particular type of writing. Then, by a show of hands, we vote on whether to place the sticky note on the right or left side of the chart.

5. After all of the sticky notes are placed, we discuss what types of visuals could be added to remind us of how these two types of writing are organized.

6. You may want to label your chart *informative* rather than *explanatory* writing. This standard uses both words for this genre. I try to deliberately move between both terms so that the students will recognize and understand them both.

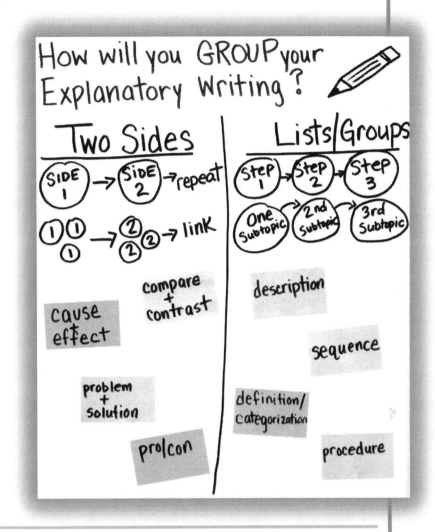

Figure 2.4 *Grouping Explanatory Writing* chart

Types of Explanatory Writing I

I typically create a version of this chart when I introduce any new genre. This is a great alternative to the prepackaged charts that list different types of writing associated with various genres. Creating this chart with students is engaging and memorable.

Creating This Chart:

1. I write the title on this chart and grab a few stacks of sticky notes to get started.

2. I tell students that there are many different types of writing that they can work on this year that inform readers. *"In fact, this type of text is all around us. Let's think of a few examples together!"*

3. I start by adding a few types to the chart. Then, I ask students to share ideas. Together, we grow the list by adding as many types as possible.

Variations:

- Consider using the term *informative* in place of *explanatory* on your chart. The standard uses both terms. You may even want to add them both to align with the standards more effectively.

- Gather examples of each type of writing. Share these with students before you create this chart. When you get ready to develop the chart, ask if students have any ideas based on the books they have just read.

- When developing this list, suggest some types of writing that are *not* accurate. Perhaps add a type of narrative to the list. See if students notice that the choice is out of place. Discuss the choice and then remove it. This is also a great moment to discuss how some types of writing can overlap and be a little bit of both. A good example is historical fiction.

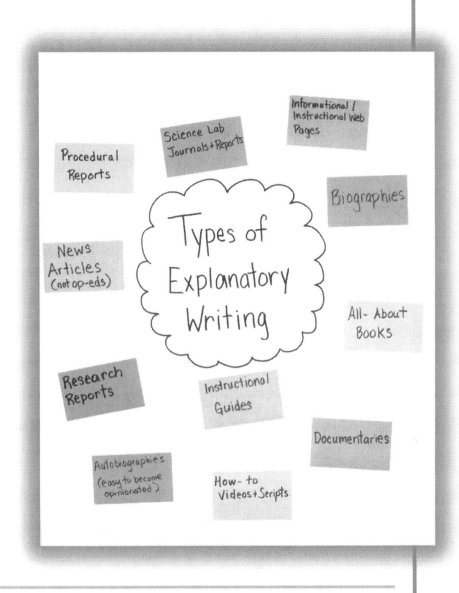

Figure 2.5 *Types of Explanatory Writing I* chart

Types of Explanatory Writing II

There are two charts in this section that bear this name. These charts were both created with different purposes in mind. The chart pictured here focuses on different ways to organize informative/ explanatory writing; while the first chart (page 66) focuses on different types and examples of informative/explanatory writing. The chart pictured here blends the learning from both standards two and four; standard four focuses on organization.

Introducing This Chart:

1. I draw the title in advance, but create the rest with students.

2. Inside of each box, I write a possible topic that could fit with each type.

3. Then, I arrange students into small groups. Each group is asked to create a topic for each type of informative writing.

4. When each group has one idea for each category, we come back together as a whole group to share the ideas. Then, I select a few and place them on the chart.

Teaching Ideas:

- Ask students to review and classify their own writing. Students can also exchange papers and classify their peers' work.

- During the small-group activity, ask students to write their own topics on the sticky notes (consider using a slightly larger size). Once the students have written down their topics, have them place them on the board. After everyone has added their topics, call on groups to try to sort the topics into the correct categories or just find all of one type and place them in a column or row. Students can take turns providing feedback to one another.

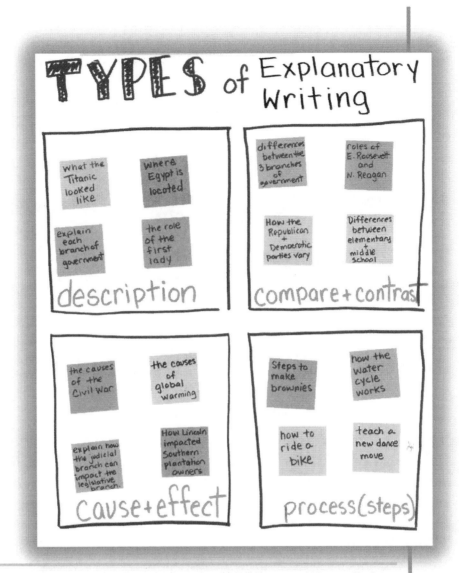

TYPES of Explanatory Writing

description
- what the Titanic looked like
- where Egypt is located
- explain each branch of government
- the role of the first lady

compare + contrast
- differences between the 3 branches of government
- roles of E. Roosevelt and N. Reagan
- How the Republican + Democratic parties vary
- Differences between elementary + middle school

cause + effect
- the causes of the Civil War
- the causes of global warming
- explain how the judicial branch can impact the legislative branch
- How Lincoln impacted Southern plantation owners

process (steps)
- Steps to make brownies
- how the water cycle works
- how to ride a bike
- teach a new dance move

Figure 2.6 *Types of Explanatory Writing II* chart

Ways to Begin an Informative Text

Leads and hooks are important to all types of writing. Different types of hooks work better with certain types of text. This chart focuses on hooks that typically work well with informative writing, but many can apply to argument/opinion writing as well.

Introducing This Chart:

1. I draw each box and name the strategy as I add it to the chart.

2. After the list is created, I ask students to help me brainstorm an image to match each strategy.

3. After the images are added, students gather their writing notebooks to select one piece of their own writing. This class had been writing how-to papers and short biographies over the past few weeks. Each student was responsible for revising the introduction for one of those papers using two different strategies from this chart.

4. While students work, I circulate around the room to answer questions and support writers.

5. At the end of the work session, students share their favorite new beginning with a small group, and three or four volunteers share with the entire class.

Variations:

- Model each strategy as you introduce it. Display these models as exemplars.

- Read excerpts from different texts that rely on each strategy.

- Add an overused strategy or one better-suited for narrative writing to the list. Explain why it is ineffective and draw a red line through it.

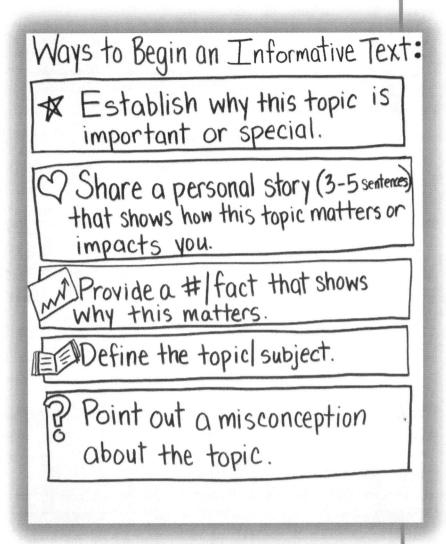

Ways to Begin an Informative Text:

☆ Establish why this topic is important or special.

♡ Share a personal story (3-5 sentences) that shows how this topic matters or impacts you.

📈 Provide a #/fact that shows why this matters.

📖 Define the topic/subject.

? Point out a misconception about the topic.

Figure 2.7 *Ways to Begin an Informative Text* chart

Ways to Build a Two-Adjective Sentence

Students seem to understand that narratives warrant rich, vivid, sensory language. Likewise, students recognize the argumentative nature of opinion writing and associate that with strong details and illustrative examples. The shift to informative writing results in papers filled with lots of sentences that sound like they have been ripped from a manual or dictionary. This chart, created with fifth graders, is designed to help students vary their sentence style when writing explanatory essays. To use this strategy for revision, refer to *Vary Your Sentences* on page 134.

Introducing This Chart:

1. I begin by drawing the columns and writing the title. At this point, I only add the heading for the *topic* column.

2. Next, I ask students to share some things that we commonly write about when we tackle explanatory writing. I add these ideas under *topic*. Note that the standard calls this informative/explanatory writing. Adjust your language based on your school requirements and preferences.

3. Then, I add the headings to the other columns and call on students to help list verbs, points, and possible adjectives. None of these lists are meant to be exhaustive; these are just representative of what we came up with that day.

4. After the chart is complete, I ask students to name a book. Once they have named the book, I follow the formula to write a sentence about that book. Next, we move to ideas. We continue down the list of topics, writing sentences to match the pattern.

Sample Two-Adjective Sentences:

- *Smart and savvy, Bill Gates is one of the world's wealthiest men.*
- *Popular and sunny, Orlando represents summer for many people.*
- *Exciting and unique, Batman: The Ride has long lines every weekend.*
- *Controversial and polarizing, the theory of evolution is taught in many schools.*

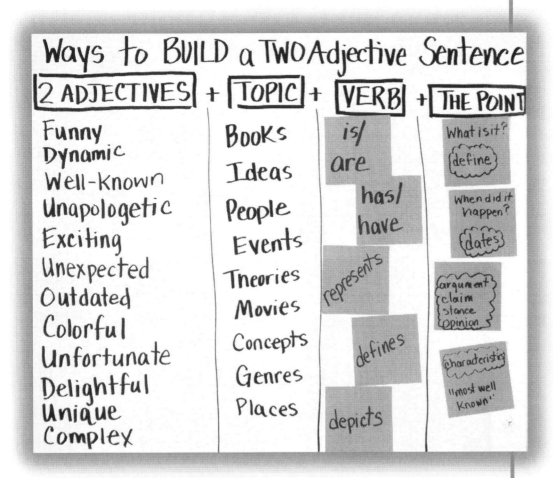

Figure 2.8 *Ways to Build a Two-Adjective Sentence* chart

Writing About Historical Events

This chart offers a roadmap for students to organize this type of essay by breaking it up into small pieces. I created this chart with a group of fifth graders, but this works for all grade levels.

Introducing This Chart:

1. I write the title and draw the steps in advance. I also prepare the categories/names of the steps in advance, but wait to add them until I am with the students.

2. I begin at the bottom left-hand corner and add the sticky note that says *the people* first. After adding the sticky note, I ask students what kind of information a reader might want to know about the people involved. We discuss possible ideas and I lead students to the three questions written next to *the people*.

3. We continue this process by listing each additional step, adding questions for each one.

4. After the chart is completed, students record the name of each step. This becomes the framework for their essay outlines.

Variations:

- These steps can serve as section headings during the initial essay drafts.

- For younger students, consider making each of the steps a different page in a book. Students could craft a paragraph and add an illustration for each page.

- Modify the steps to be as specific or as broad as you like. This can help you guide or direct your students to focus on any aspect of informative/explanatory writing that you want to target.

- Use the terms as categories for a rubric or checklist.

Figure 2.9 *Writing About Historical Events* chart

Writing About People

While writing topics vary widely, you can count on the fact that just about every student, at some point in his or her school career, will be asked to craft an essay about a person. Since this is an inevitability, teaching students how to write about people makes a lot of sense. This chart, while seemingly simple, is the response to the infamous, *"I can't think of anything else to write!"*

Creating This Chart:

1. Before planning to write about a fictitious or real person, I ask students to think about what makes a person. *"What pieces build who we are or who anyone is?"*

2. The most common initial responses include "family" and "physical appearance."

3. I continue to probe and drop hints to encourage a wider variety of responses. Then, I start to add the things that students share to the chart.

4. Finally, I tell students that these are the types of things that we can write about when we tell about a person.

Variations:

• Draw a puzzle to create this chart. Fill in each of the puzzle pieces with one of the categories from the chart. This goes nicely with the idea that these are the "pieces" that make up a person.

• Ask students to organize this list from most important to least important. Students can write down their lists to use as a guide when they are selecting what headings to include in their own writing. This will really help with organization.

• Before crafting a full essay, students can write short paragraphs to describe a person. Students simply select what they want to include from the list. If their writing is choppy, require students to not only include the type of detail, but follow it up with a second sentence to explain the significance of the detail.

Figure 2.10 *Writing About People* chart

Chart Sense for Writing   www.ChartSense.RozLinder.com

Chapter 3

Narratives

Common Core Writing Anchor Standard 3:

Write narratives to develop real or imagined experiences or events using effective technique, well-chosen details, and well-structured event sequences.

3

Write narratives to develop real or imagined experiences or events using effective technique, descriptive details, and clear event sequences.
a. Establish a situation and introduce a narrator and/or characters; organize an event sequence that unfolds naturally.
b. Use dialogue and descriptions of actions, thoughts, and feelings to develop experiences and events or show the response of characters to situations.
c. Use temporal words and phrases to signal event order.
d. Provide a sense of closure.

4

Write narratives to develop real or imagined experiences or events using effective technique, descriptive details, and clear event sequences.
a. Orient the reader by establishing a situation and introducing a narrator and/or characters; organize an event sequence that unfolds naturally.
b. Use dialogue and description to develop experiences and events or show the responses of characters to situations.
c. Use a variety of transitional words and phrases to manage the sequence of events.
d. Use concrete words and phrases and sensory details to convey experiences and events precisely.
e. Provide a conclusion that follows from the narrated experiences or events.

5

Write narratives to develop real or imagined experiences or events using effective technique, descriptive details, and clear event sequences.
a. Orient the reader by establishing a situation and introducing a narrator and/or characters; organize an event sequence that unfolds naturally.
b. Use narrative techniques, such as dialogue, description, and pacing, to develop experiences and events or show the responses of characters to situations.
c. Use a variety of transitional words, phrases, and clauses to manage the sequence of events.
d. Use concrete words and phrases and sensory details to convey experiences and events precisely.
e. Provide a conclusion that follows from the narrated experiences or events.

6

Write narratives to develop real or imagined experiences or events using effective technique, relevant descriptive details, and well-structured event sequences.
a. Engage and orient the reader by establishing a context and introducing a narrator and/or characters; organize an event sequence that unfolds naturally and logically.
b. Use narrative techniques, such as dialogue, pacing, and description, to develop experiences, events, and/or characters.
c. Use a variety of transition words, phrases, and clauses to convey sequence and signal shifts from one time frame or setting to another.
d. Use precise words and phrases, relevant descriptive details, and sensory language to convey experiences and events.
e. Provide a conclusion that follows from the narrated experiences or events.

7

Write narratives to develop real or imagined experiences or events using effective technique, relevant descriptive details, and well-structured event sequences.
a. Engage and orient the reader by establishing a context and point of view and introducing a narrator and/or characters; organize an event sequence that unfolds naturally and logically.
b. Use narrative techniques, such as dialogue, pacing, and description, to develop experiences, events, and/or characters.
c. Use a variety of transition words, phrases, and clauses to convey sequence and signal shifts from one time frame or setting to another.
d. Use precise words and phrases, relevant descriptive details, and sensory language to capture the action and convey experiences and events.
e. Provide a conclusion that follows from and reflects on the narrated experiences or events.

8

Write narratives to develop real or imagined experiences or events using effective technique, relevant descriptive details, and well-structured event sequences.
a. Engage and orient the reader by establishing a context and point of view and introducing a narrator and/or characters; organize an event sequence that unfolds naturally and logically.
b. Use narrative techniques, such as dialogue, pacing, description, and reflection, to develop experiences, events, and/or characters.
c. Use a variety of transition words, phrases, and clauses to convey sequence, signal shifts from one time frame or setting to another, and show the relationships among experiences and events.
d. Use precise words and phrases, relevant descriptive details, and sensory language to capture the action and convey experiences and events.
e. Provide a conclusion that follows from and reflects on the narrated experiences or events.

Adjectives can Compare

Standard three asks students to use descriptive details in their narratives. One of the most comfortable and familiar ways for students to do this is with adjectives. Unfortunately, adjectives are regularly misused when students use them to compare. This chart is a simple reminder to use *more* or add an *–er* when comparing two things and to use *most* or *–est* with more than two.

Creating This Chart:

1. I begin by calling two students to the front of the room. I ask students how I would compare their heights to one another. Typically, someone will say that one student is taller than the other.

2. I add *taller* to the chart, leaving space for the large sticky note that will come later.

3. Next, I call a third student to the front of the room. Again, I ask how I could compare their heights. Some students will still say that one student is taller. I draw attention to the *–er* at the end of *taller* and point out that this only works with groups of two. Unless I am grouping the two students as a collective, I have three separate entities here.

4. When a student finally suggests *tallest*, I add this to the list.

5. We continue this process with other objects and images in the room (photographs, books, fictitious characters, etc.).

6. Finally, I add the large sticky notes and explain the terms *comparative* and *superlative*.

Teaching Ideas:

- Send students on a book scavenger hunt. Challenge students to find narratives that use the comparative or superlative forms of adjectives. Ask students to share their findings in small groups.

- Have students take the words on the chart and create sentences that compare objects accurately.

- Ask students to work in groups to add more comparative and superlative adjectives to the chart.

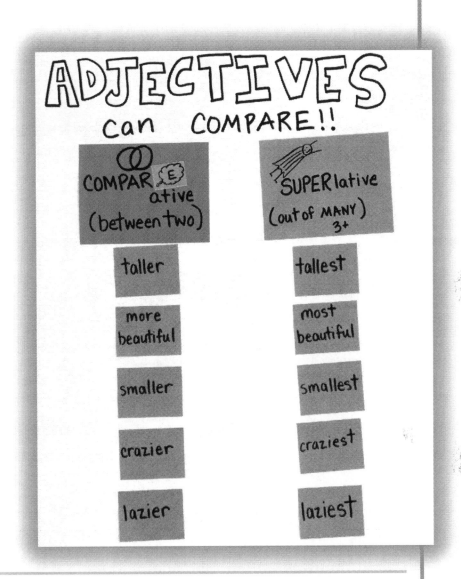

Figure 3.1 *Adjectives Can Compare* chart

Create a Narrative Scene

I created this chart with a group of third graders. This fun chart helped students to organize their narrative events in a logical order that was easy to follow.

Teaching With This Chart:

1. Students had already planned their narratives using story maps and plot diagrams (student choice). Each student had a different set of events that they wanted to write about. This chart was to help them to develop those individual moments.

2. I placed each of the four sticky notes on the chart and explained each one.

3. *"First, you have to let readers know where you are. You can tell us or give a hint, but take some time to situate the location."* Students can name where the story is physically set or where it is in time and space.

4. For the second sticky note, students use sensory language to create a visual for readers. This could be a continuation of the setting description or it could shift to the character(s). Regardless, this is where readers can close their eyes and imagine this world. For more skilled writers, these first two sticky notes can be combined into one step. For less proficient writers, I keep these as two different steps.

5. The third sticky note is where the moment begins to unfold. This is the heart of what this moment is about. I find that this is the easiest one for students. Simplicity actually works well here because students have already set up the scene through the other two steps.

6. The final sticky note is where you get the most bang for your buck! Most writers want to trail off and end after they unfold the event. Instead, I ask students to let the characters or narrator think out loud. *"What do you wonder? What do you hope or wish? Reflect on this moment."* This can be one sentence, but it is a powerful conclusion to a narrative moment.

7. As students move on to the next moment, they can repeat this process. Going back to step one means establishing the next setting or context. This is where they transition and move through the next event.

Figure 3.2 *Create a Narrative Scene* chart

Develop Settings and Characters

This checklist was created with fifth graders working on realistic fiction pieces. We were fleshing out our character and setting descriptions, but students were only describing the physical appearances and what they could see on the outside. I wanted them to go deeper and think about how many different elements really make up a character or a setting.

Introducing This Chart:

1. I draw the images on large sticky notes in advance. Then, I begin by reading this description: *"Tracy was taller than the other girls in her class. She had curly black hair and red glasses."*

2. I ask, *"What do you guys think? Did you recognize any description there?"* Students usually all agree that the writer uses some describing words.

3. Then, I read this sentence: *"When Charles smiled, his mouth seemed to have too many teeth and his chubby cheeks squished his eyes shut."* The students will agree that this sentence is better and also includes description.

4. *"These descriptions are fabulous, but what are they isolated to?"* I call on students until someone explains that they each focus on what people look like.

5. I explain that our new goal is to move our description beyond just the surface. *"Tell me more than just the outside. How does Tracy feel? What is she known for? Drop descriptive hints that not only tell me the outside, but give me a peek on the inside."*

6. Then, I begin adding the checkboxes and discussing each one. *"When you write, see if you can check off a few of these. Now I don't want these all packed into one or two sentences, but sprinkle them throughout. Reveal bits and pieces as you write. When you are stuck and need more, look at this chart and see if you can add rich description by describing one of these elements."*

7. With that, I send students off to dig through their notebooks to find places in their writing where they can flesh out characters or expand settings.

8. If this list is too overwhelming, introduce and model just a few at a time.

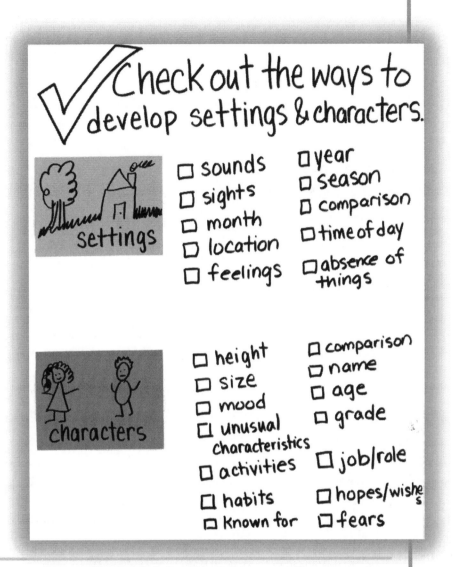

Check out the ways to develop settings & characters.

settings
- ☐ sounds
- ☐ sights
- ☐ month
- ☐ location
- ☐ feelings
- ☐ year
- ☐ season
- ☐ comparison
- ☐ time of day
- ☐ absence of things

characters
- ☐ height
- ☐ size
- ☐ mood
- ☐ unusual characteristics
- ☐ activities
- ☐ habits
- ☐ known for
- ☐ comparison
- ☐ name
- ☐ age
- ☐ grade
- ☐ job/role
- ☐ hopes/wishes
- ☐ fears

Figure 3.3 *Develop Settings and Characters* chart

LOOK for
Adverbs and Adjectives

Rich description is a central part of narrative writing, but can be applicable to any type of writing. This chart, created with fifth graders, is designed to break up some of the monotonous description that students tend to rely on.

Introducing This Chart:

1. I begin by asking students how they add description to their writing. Students typically share ideas like: sensory language, adverbs, adjectives, and vivid words.

2. I explain that today I want to share a method of placing adjectives and adverbs in different locations for sentence variety.

3. At this point, I write the title on the chart and begin writing about Gina. *"This is from a story that I have been working on about a character named Gina who is really nervous about giving a big speech. She is a bit hesitant to talk in front of a large crowd."*

4. After I write, I underline four sections and point out that I intentionally put my adverbs and adjectives in these places.

5. Then, I ask students how they would describe the placement of these words. We discuss different ways to name what I had done. I then draw the arrows to point to the name of the strategy. The goal is that students recognize the placement and replicate it in their own writing.

6. Finally, I ask students to take out the writing that they have been doing this week and look for subjects and verbs within their stories. *"Guys, find at least one place to try out each of these strategies."*

7. I usually set a timer to create a sense of urgency. Typically fifteen minutes is enough for most students to make several revisions. After the timer goes off, students share their changes with the class.

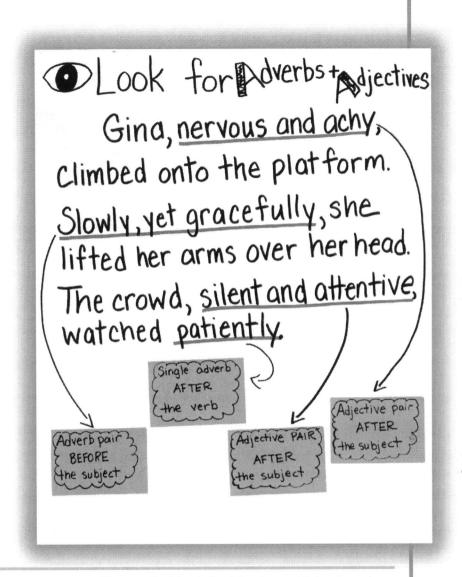

Figure 3.4 *Look for Adverbs and Adjectives* chart

Narrative Endings

This chart was created with sixth graders. Students had written personal narratives during the week. Most of the students had written full stories, but typically just ended the narrative with the last event or big moment. While many of the stories had great arcs, the endings felt more like letdowns. The students needed to tie the stories up in ways that were more meaningful. I created this chart to help them with that.

Creating This Chart:

I write this entire chart with the students. I simply name the strategy and list it. I tell students that they can easily use one or two of these to wrap up their stories in a more powerful way. Then, I ask students to think about which narrative ending they want to try out. We talk about their ideas, then I group students together based on their choices. Students who want to end with a lesson learned can be grouped together. Students who want to mirror their leads can be seated together. Of course there are always some outliers and students who will move amongst the groups. Students try out different endings and share them with their group members for feedback.

Teaching Tips:

- Consider sharing narratives that mirror these types of endings with students.

- If your class has been working on a shared piece of writing, consider introducing this chart right before you craft the ending and work together to try out several different endings.

- Ask students to write two different narrative endings and compare them. Next, students can get peer feedback and choose which one works best. This is a great moment to talk about audience awareness as well. For more on audience awareness, see the charts in chapter four.

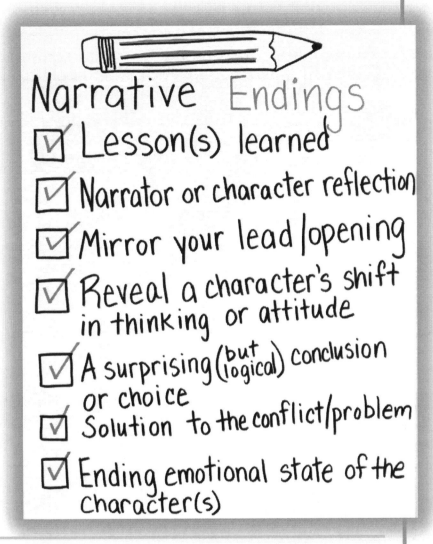

Narrative Endings
- ☑ Lesson(s) learned
- ☑ Narrator or character reflection
- ☑ Mirror your lead/opening
- ☑ Reveal a character's shift in thinking or attitude
- ☑ A surprising (but logical) conclusion or choice
- ☑ Solution to the conflict/problem
- ☑ Ending emotional state of the character(s)

Figure 3.5 *Narrative Endings* chart

Organize Your Narrative

This chart was developed during a fiction unit. Third graders were creating narrative picture books. This same chart would work just as effectively for essay-style narratives for older students.

Creating This Chart:

1. I write the chart title and the first step. I explain that we are going to develop a story that follows one of these four plot lines: *character versus character, character versus nature, lost and found,* or *character versus himself.* I add small sticky notes after I describe each one. Some teachers add *character versus society* instead of *lost and found.* Vary these based on your personal preferences. For a chart that teaches these four types in greater detail, refer to the chart called *Story Types* on page 92.

2. I continue through the chart, describing each step. For step two, I write different types of possible challenges on colored page markers. If you are not familiar with page markers, refer to page 24.

3. After we complete the chart, I place large sticky notes around the room that have either *character versus character, character versus nature, lost and found,* or *character versus himself* written on them. Students are asked to go to the corner that has the plot line that they find the most interesting. Students are able to visit as many corners as they want to. Each corner houses a small collection of picture books that match that plot structure. Students can spend the rest of the period reading and exploring the different books. For my extensive list of picture books that match each type of plot structure and a color image of this chart, visit me online at: http://ontheweb.rozlinder.com/narrative-writing-organization.

4. The next day, students can share the plot that they have selected. Then, they are able to decide who their main characters will be.

5. Once this is done, students follow the steps to create a plan for their narratives.

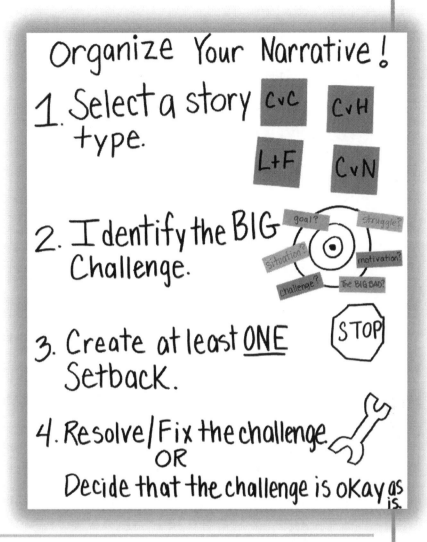

Figure 3.6 *Organize Your Narrative chart*

Story Types

This chart was created with a group of third graders. We used the chart during both reading to explore different plots. Later, we relied on this same information when we moved to crafting our own narratives.

Introducing This Chart:

I draw each image in front of the students and add each one to the chart. Then, I read a picture book out loud to the students. They then try to guess which story (plot) type the book follows. When the students name a story type, I ask them to explain how they guessed. As they explain, I add the bullets under the sticky note. After all four books had been read, I ask students to record these four types of stories in the writing folders to help encourage future story ideas.

Teaching Tips:

1. In retrospect, *character versus himself* should probably have been renamed to the gender-neutral *character versus self.*

2. *Lost and found* stories can also include stories where a character is lost and searching for a way home. I didn't add that on our list, but it is important and should have been included. *Baby Bear* on the book list below is a story like that.

Books With Different Story Types:

- *Baby Bear* by Kadir Nelson (lost and found)

- *Brave Irene* by William Steig (character versus nature)

- *Fiona's Luck* by Teresa Bateman (character versus character)

- *Game Day* by Tiki and Ronde Barber (character versus himself)

- *Harriet and the Promised Land* by Jacob Lawrence (character versus character)

- *I Want my Hat Back* by Jon Klassen (lost and found)

- *Ming Lo Moves the Mountain* by Arnold Lobel (character versus nature)

- *Papi's Gift* by Karen Stanton (character versus himself)

- *Stella Louella's Runaway Book* by Lisa Campbell Ernst (lost and found)

STORY TYPES — Which type will you write?

Character v. Himself

- overcoming fears
- self-esteem issues
- learning a lesson
- transformation

Character v. Nature

- natural disaster
- survival story
- animal v. man

Lost & Found

- lost valuables
- lost item w/ consequences
- lost item where time is a factor

Character v. Character

- bad guys + good guys
- bullies
- archenemies
- competitors

Figure 3.7 *Story Types* chart

Transitions
Help Your Writing

Throughout this book I mention the different ways that the writing standards overlap or are interrelated. This is particularly true when it comes to transitional words. The only places where the word *transition* is actually mentioned in the writing standards is within the narrative and explanatory strand. This strikes me as odd because transitions are used in all types of writing. Because transitions are specifically named in the narrative writing standard, I have included this chart here, but it can be used with all types of writing. To adhere to the language of the standard, there is also a transition chart found in the section on explanatory writing called *Six Types of Transitions* on page 52. A shorter chart, *Don't be a Bore*, can be found on page 108.

Introducing This Chart:

1. I write the title in advance, but add the information on the sticky notes with the students.

2. After I explain each one, I add the sentence starters for each type of transition under the name of that transition.

3. Next, I have students reread one of their older pieces of writing and find at least two places where they can add or revise a transition.

4. After students work on this, I call on volunteers to share the sentence in front of the transition, along with the sentence that follows the transition.

5. As each student reads, the others listen and raise their hands to try to name the type of transition that they notice in the paper being read aloud. We discuss the changes and even consider other revisions.

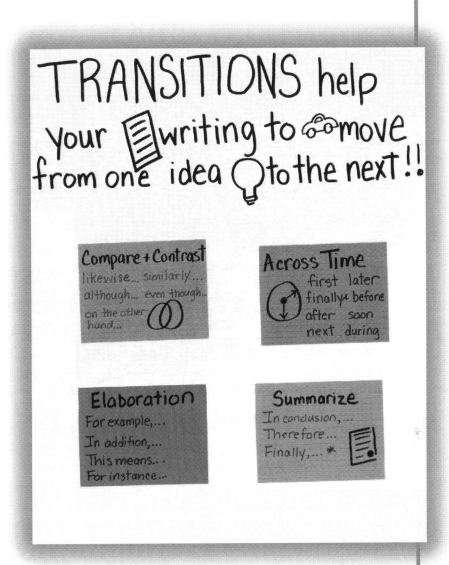

Figure 3.8 *Transition Helps Your Writing* chart

Types of Hooks

This fun chart was created with fifth graders. Many students try to use the same strategies to craft narrative hooks/leads as they use to craft explanatory leads. This is problematic because those types of hooks can seem forced when used to introduce a story.

Creating This Chart:

1. I begin by displaying several books on a table in front of the classroom.

2. Then, I draw the hook and title on the chart. For a better-looking chart, consider creating the hook in advance.

3. Next, I group students into pairs. I ask each pair to work as a team to explore the books on the table. *"Guys, with your partners, look at how these authors crafted their beginnings."*

4. As students read, I circulate around the room, leading them to possible ideas.

5. Afterwards, we list the types of hooks that we noticed on sticky notes and place them on the chart.

6. After this chart picture was taken a few changes were made. I changed *Emotional Statement* to *Emotional Triggers*. We felt that this was a better description of what we found in books. Later, we added a new type of hook called a *mirror hook*. This is when the exact sentence begins and ends the book (i.e. Kevin Henke's *Sheila Rae* and Cynthia Rylant's *The Relatives Came*).

My Favorite Display Books:

- *A Mango-Shaped Space* by Wendy Mass (conversation)
- *Goggles* by Ezra Jack Keats (conversation)
- *Harry Potter and the Sorcerer's Stone* by J.K. Rowling (character description)
- *How My Parents Learned to Eat* by Ina Friedman (flashback)
- *How to Eat Fried Worms* by Thomas Rockwell (conversation)
- *Love, Ruby Lavender* by Deborah Wiles (begins with a character speaking, but it is so emotionally charged that it works for an emotional trigger)
- *Matilda* by Roald Dahl (unexpected statement/emotional trigger)
- *Owl Moon* by Jane Yolen (setting)
- *So B. It* by Sarah Weeks (character thinking)
- *The Landry News* by Andrew Clements (character description)
- *The Last Treasure* by Janet Anderson (setting and character description)

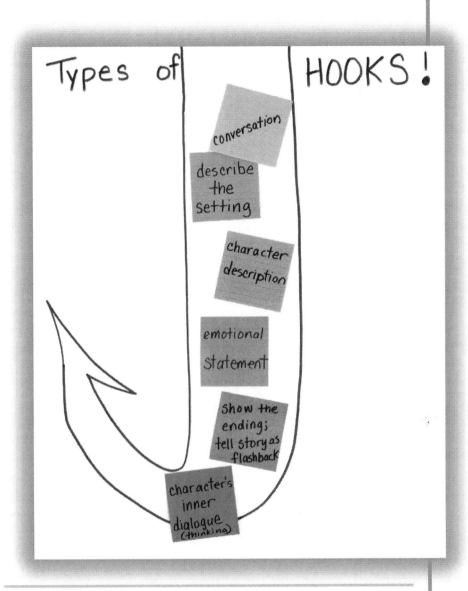

Figure 3.9 *Types of Hooks* chart

Using Dialogue

This chart, created with fifth graders, features four different guidelines to help students organize dialogue.

Introducing This Chart:

1. I begin with only the speech bubble and title written on this chart.

2. I ask students if they have ever written about characters who talk to each other. *"How do you do it? What do you put on paper to show that characters are saying things?"*

3. Students typically share ideas about quotation marks and indenting. They all have some type of general understanding of how dialogue works.

4. At this point, I introduce the purpose of the lesson. *"Today we will take a look at a few rules that we have to follow when using speech in our stories."*

5. Next, I add the large sticky notes and explain each one.

Dialogue Rules:

- The first sticky note (top left) explains that punctuation goes before the ending quotation mark. There are also two additional smaller sticky notes that point out that the speech tag can come first, followed by the actual direct speech. The second small sticky note shows that students can reverse this process and add the direct speech first, followed by the speech tag. The boxes illustrate possible punctuation marks, depending on which order students select.

- The second large sticky note (top right) explains that any dialogue introduced with the word *that* is not direct speech and doesn't require quotation marks.

- The third sticky note (bottom left) illustrates a method of splitting a line of direct speech by inserting the speech tag in the middle. An example is showcased in the box below.

- The final sticky note (bottom right) explains that a new speaker warrants a new paragraph.

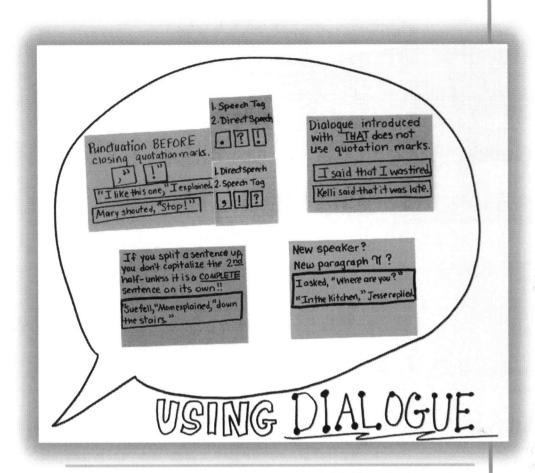

Figure 3.10 *Using Dialogue* chart

Types of Narrative Writing

This simple chart is a great tool to transition to narrative writing from other genres. I created this particular chart with fifth graders to kick off a narrative unit.

Teaching With This Chart:

1. I simply draw the title and ask students to name different types of narrative writing that they are familiar with. As students share, we generate this list by adding their ideas to the chart.

2. After the chart is filled with their ideas, I group students into teams of three. Each team selects a type of narrative writing. I remove oral history from the list, and a few other categories may be left over, depending on the size of the class.

3. Next, I like to take a trip to the media center. I ask students to locate narrative examples that match the sticky note that they have.

4. When we return to the class, students can share their findings.

Variations:

- For a more time-efficient trip to the media center, ask your media specialist to pull books in advance and place them on a cart or central location. Students can congregate here, rather than roam the media center.

- Split this into a two-day activity and focus on a few types each day.

- If you have a small class, assign groups more than one type of narrative writing to look for.

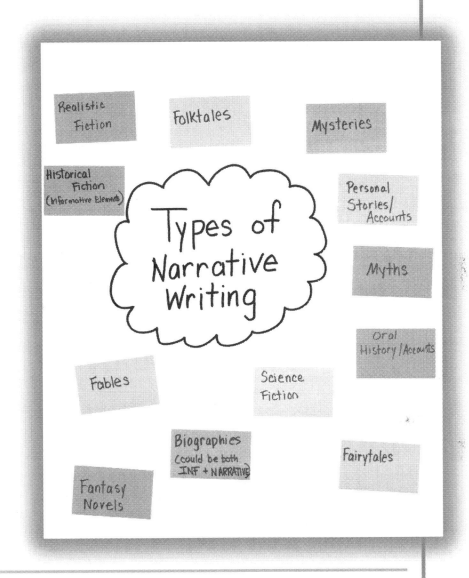

Realistic Fiction

Folktales

Mysteries

Historical Fiction (Informative Element)

Personal Stories/ Accounts

Types of Narrative Writing

Myths

Oral History/Accounts

Fables

Science Fiction

Biographies (could be both INF + NARRATIVE)

Fairytales

Fantasy Novels

Figure 3.11 *Types of Narrative Writing* chart

Chapter 4

Organization & Style

Common Core Writing Anchor Standard 4:

Produce clear and coherent writing in which the development, organization, and style are appropriate to task, purpose, and audience.

3	With guidance and support from adults, produce writing in which the development and organization are appropriate to task and purpose. (Grade-specific expectations for writing types are defined in standards 1–3.)
4	Produce clear and coherent writing in which the development and organization are appropriate to task, purpose, and audience. (Grade-specific expectations for writing types are defined in standards 1–3.)
5	Produce clear and coherent writing in which the development and organization are appropriate to task, purpose, and audience. (Grade-specific expectations for writing types are defined in standards 1–3.)
6	Produce clear and coherent writing in which the development and organization are appropriate to task, purpose, and audience. (Grade-specific expectations for writing types are defined in standards 1–3.)
7	Produce clear and coherent writing in which the development and organization are appropriate to task, purpose, and audience. (Grade-specific expectations for writing types are defined in standards 1–3.)
8	Produce clear and coherent writing in which the development and organization are appropriate to task, purpose, and audience. (Grade-specific expectations for writing types are defined in standards 1–3.)

Check Your Paragraphs

This chart was created with fifth graders to help organize their writing. Students in virtually every grade level can benefit from a variation of this chart.

Creating This Chart:

I simply write the title and list each type of organization next to the boxes. As I add each idea, I stop to explain the meaning. When I created this chart, students had already been introduced to organizational structures through reading, so this lesson served more as a connection between reading and writing.

Variations:

- Consider adding a corresponding image next to each one.

- Write the different types of organizational structures on large sticky notes. Only add the ones that you want students to focus on at different points throughout the year.

- Read paragraphs and ask students to identify how the paragraphs are organized. Use this as a formative assessment.

- When students complete essay drafts, ask them to label how different sections are organized within their own writing.

- Type this up into a smaller chart that students can use as a bookmark or keep in their writing folders.

- Add this chart to any revision and editing stations/centers in your classroom.

- During peer editing, encourage students to ask about how and why sections are organized. The more students are cognizant of organizational styles, the more they can vary their own.

✓ Check Your Paragraphs π

☐ cause/effect
☐ time sequence
☐ compare / contrast
☐ flashback (deliberately out of
            sequence)
☐ list | qualities / traits

Is your organization
clear and consistent???

Figure 4.1 *Check Your Paragraphs* chart

Different Audiences . . .

Audience awareness is an area of writing that students easily overlook or ignore. Attention to audience is identified in this standard, but also embedded in each of the writing standards. For seventh- and eighth-grade students, standard five (revision) also asks students to focus on audience.

Introducing This Chart:

1. I introduce this chart to students by asking them who they have written to or for. As students share ideas, I probe and ask more questions about the type of writing that they have done and for what purposes.

2. After hearing about the different audiences students have written for, I pull out the chart materials and add the title to the chart.

3. I explain that the people that they just named are all *audience members.*

4. As I add the large sticky notes to the chart, I really focus on the notion that these ideas are all driven by the different types of audiences that students had just shared with me. *"You guys just told me that writers change their writing styles based on their audience and purpose. Check out all of the different audiences we have when we write!"*

5. At the bottom of the chart, I list some of the ways that writing changes based on the audience.

6. After creating this chart, I call on volunteers to select two different audiences from the chart. Then, the student volunteers share at least one way that their writing would vary if they were writing for each of the two different audiences. This is a simple activity that can be repeated as many times as possible.

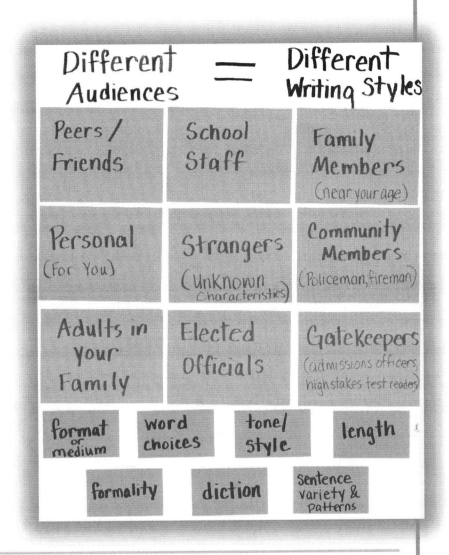

Figure 4.2 *Different Audiences ... chart*

Don't Be a Bore!

Transitions are heavily embedded in most of the writing standards. Students who are used to very traditional five-paragraph essays tend to use transitions that are robotic and dry. This chart introduces students to a wider variety of transitions that work well with most types of writing. For transitions that focus more on narrative writing, see *Transitions Help Your Writing* on page 94.

Introducing This Chart:

1. I draw the title and tell students that we want to avoid boring transitions. *"Let's see if we can stop using first, second, and third in our writing."*

2. While this was just a small step, it was the beginning of students considering other ways to transition to new ideas. *"Why don't we test drive some other ideas for transitions?"*

3. At this point, I draw the first set of transitions on the chart. *"Who would consider using these three?"*

4. Students typically nod and a few raise their hands. I continue through the list in a similar manner.

5. At the end of the list, I ask students to look at their earlier essays and find places with a "boring" transition and revise it with one from our chart.

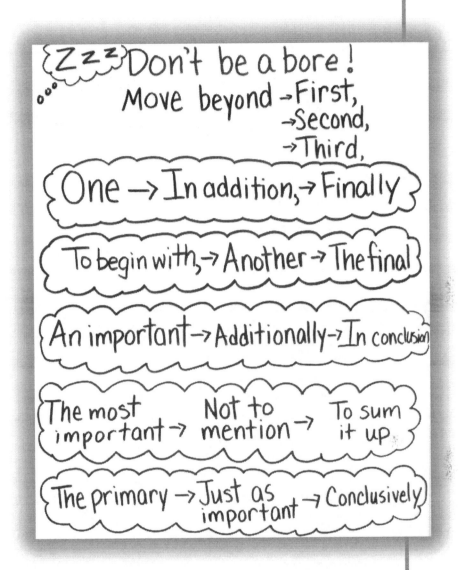

Figure 4.3 *Don't Be a Bore!* chart

Three-Part Leads

The writing standards overlap a lot! This chart touches on so many other standards that it could definitely fit in multiple chapters. At the core, this chart is about developing an effective hook or lead. This puts it squarely in the domain of development and organization, yet it could also be taught with either the explanatory or argument standards. Keep this in mind as you teach different standards. They will and do overlap. No writing standards exist in isolation. For narrative-specific leads, see *Types of Hooks* on page 96. For argument-specific leads, see *Reasons to Begin with Multiple Questions* on page 50 and *This is Hard* on page 54.

Introducing This Chart:

1. I had previously given a group of fifth graders a list of ideas for crafting hooks. One of the ideas on the list had been to simply write three words or three sentences that mirrored one another. The results were disastrous! Students were grouping random words together and they were almost comical.

2. I gathered students together and wrote *Historic. President. Voting.* This was an actual excerpt from a student's paper who attempted to use this strategy. I asked students why this didn't work, and we added a few ideas to the list.

3. Next, I wrote three alternatives on the chart. We discussed why these worked better. Then, I added arrows to point to the reasons why these three-part leads were more effective than the example at the top.

4. Finally, I reminded students that three-part leads didn't always work for every piece. Don't force a lead when it doesn't fit. *"The whole point of having different strategies is to use what is most effective. Slapping three words on a paper and calling that a hook is the easy way out. Go with what works, not with what's fastest."*

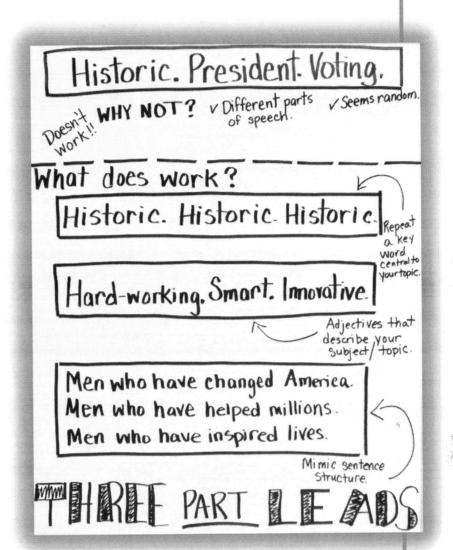

Figure 4.4 *Three-Part Leads* chart

Want Clear Writing?

This standard asks students to pay close attention to *task*, *audience*, and *purpose*. Often these three words show up on scoring rubrics and checklists, but rarely is much time devoted to really delving into what they mean. This chart, created with third graders, is designed to make these ideas clearer and to provide guiding questions. Students are able to assess if they have developed their writing appropriately for the audience, task, and designated purpose.

Introducing This Chart:

1. I begin by writing the title at the top of the chart. Then, I ask the students if it really matters if our writing is clear. *"Guys, don't you want clear writing? If your writing isn't clear, no one will understand what you're trying to say!"* Most students will nod in agreement.

2. *"Well, to be clear, you need to think about three different things."* I add each of the three large sticky notes to the chart and call on a student to read each one aloud.

3. I remind them, *"These are always at the center of everything that we write. Whether you write a narrative, opinion, or explanatory piece —these three things always matter."*

4. After reinforcing the importance of these three areas, I start to add the questions next to *task*. After I write and explain each one, I ask a volunteer to explain what he or she would do when thinking about that question.

5. Finally, this chart is typically hung over the editing station. Students are asked to refer to the questions during both planning and revision.

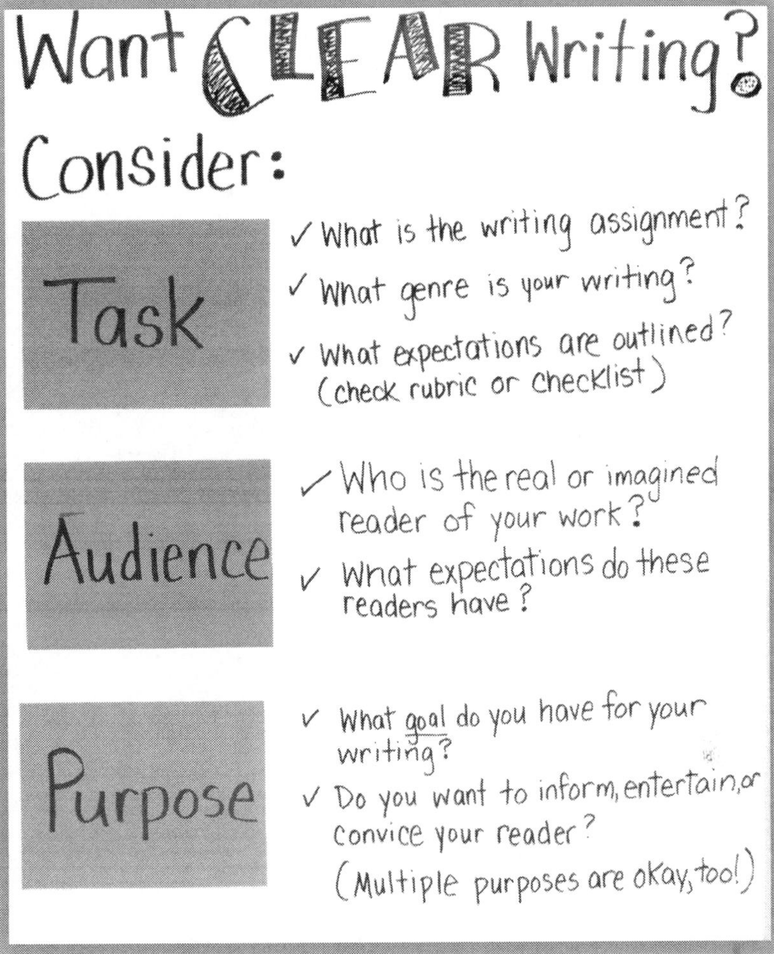

Want CLEAR Writing?

Consider:

Task
- ✓ What is the writing assignment?
- ✓ What genre is your writing?
- ✓ What expectations are outlined? (check rubric or checklist)

Audience
- ✓ Who is the real or imagined reader of your work?
- ✓ What expectations do these readers have?

Purpose
- ✓ What goal do you have for your writing?
- ✓ Do you want to inform, entertain, or convice your reader? (Multiple purposes are okay, too!)

Figure 4.5 *Want Clear Writing?* chart

What is the Best Format for Your Writing?

This chart, created with fourth graders, mirrors the learning of reading standard five (text features). In reading, students are asked to use features to gather information and learn. For the writing standard, students are asked to think about the best way to organize their own writing. To do this effectively, students need to know what formats exist and ask questions about which ones make the most sense for their audiences and purposes.

Introducing This Chart:

I begin by asking students which organizational formats they already know about, adding each one to the chart. When students run out of ideas, I provide some other examples. Then, I explain that what really matters is not that we use a lot of different formats; what matters is that we select formats that make the most sense for our writing. We talk about choices that would be silly or ineffective for certain audiences or purposes. We also talk about formats that work well for different tasks. For example, numbered lists make sense for a how-to book, but not so much for a narrative fairytale.

Teaching Ideas:

- If you teach both reading and writing, plan this unit to coincide with the introduction of reading standard five. Select texts that provide strong examples of these features to explore during reading time. During writing time, ask students to mirror this type of writing.

- Have students identify a small chunk of their writing, maybe a paragraph or several sentences. Ask them to represent the information in two different formats, then discuss the advantages and disadvantages of each. Remember that traditional paragraphs (while not listed on the chart) still count as a format and choice.

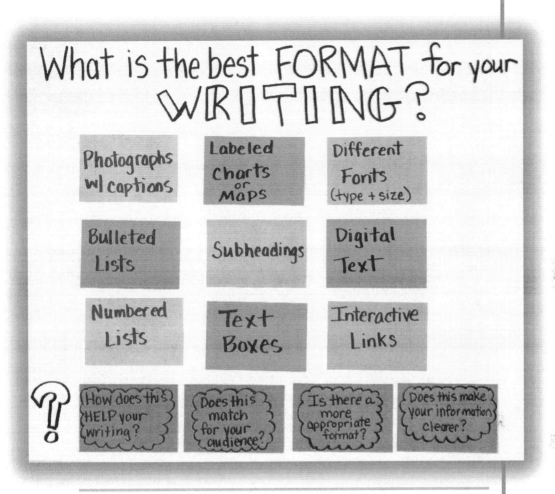

Figure 4.6 *What is the Best Format for Your Writing?* chart

When to Start a New Paragraph

This chart was created with fifth graders. The students had just finished a unit on opinion writing and were days into a unit on narrative writing. The goal for this lesson was to prevent writing with one indentation for the whole paper or lots of random paragraphs, with no logical reason for paragraph breaks.

Introducing This Chart:

1. I gather students together and write the title of the chart. *"Guys, how do you know when to start a new paragraph?"*

2. Responses are usually varied and will include comments like: *when you have too much in that paragraph, enough to get five paragraphs, when you tell us to,* and *after five sentences.*

3. I explain that there are actually some rules to think about when starting a new paragraph. *"Well, I am going to clear this up and teach you guys the rules so that you always know when to start a new paragraph."*

4. I add all of the sticky notes to the chart and ask students to take a moment to read them silently and think about each one.

5. After a minute or two, I call on a volunteer to read each one out loud. Then, we discuss each, matching them to specific genres.

Variations:

- Make this list match your students! For example, notice that I did not include *New Topic* on this list. That is a common and very valid reason to start a new paragraph. Because we were moving to narrative writing, I knew that they needed more story-based reasons to transition, so I leaned more in that direction. I also knew that they had focused a lot on providing examples and evidence in their previous unit on opinion writing, so I led with reasons typically used in opinion writing first.

- Share examples from books or online articles that start paragraphs in the same ways that you describe on the list.

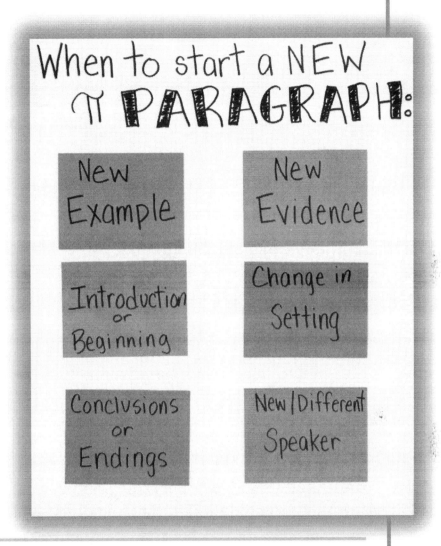

Figure 4.7 *When to Start a New Paragraph* chart

Chapter 5

Revision & Editing

Common Core Writing Anchor Standard 5:

Develop and strengthen writing as needed by planning, revising, editing, rewriting, or trying a new approach.

3 With guidance and support from peers and adults, develop and strengthen writing as needed by planning, revising, and editing.

4 With guidance and support from peers and adults, develop and strengthen writing as needed by planning, revising, and editing.

5 With guidance and support from peers and adults, develop and strengthen writing as needed by planning, revising, editing, rewriting, or trying a new approach.

6 With some guidance and support from peers and adults, develop and strengthen writing as needed by planning, revising, editing, rewriting, or trying a new approach.

7 With some guidance and support from peers and adults, develop and strengthen writing as needed by planning, revising, editing, rewriting, or trying a new approach, focusing on how well purpose and audience have been addressed.

8 With some guidance and support from peers and adults, develop and strengthen writing as needed by planning, revising, editing, rewriting, or trying a new approach, focusing on how well purpose and audience have been addressed.

Do I Need to Revise?

This chart was created in reaction to a bit of frustration that I felt when working with a group of fourth graders. After the students had written rough drafts, they were willing to edit for capitalization and grammar. When it came to revision, they seemed stuck. The students did not understand how or when to revise.

Preparation for This Chart:

To create this chart, I sifted through student writing journals to find sentences that were vague or nonspecific. I recorded these sentences on large sticky notes in advance. Next, I jotted down a few different ways that I could revise each sentence. I planned to have students generate these possibilities, but having a few to reference was critical in case students struggled with examples.

Introducing This Chart:

I begin by just writing the title on the chart. I explain that writers revise to help readers picture their ideas more clearly. To do this, students should reread their sentences and ask if they can picture the information clearly. Is the information fuzzy? Is it vague? If students have a hard time pinpointing the meaning, perhaps revision is needed. Next, we look at the sentences on the sticky notes, then spend time talking through ways to make each one better. These new sentences are recorded on large sticky notes and placed at the bottom of the chart.

Extension Ideas:

- Rather than fuzzy and unclear, consider asking students if their language is precise, specific, vague, or too broad. Use terms that match any rubrics or checklists that you use.
- Challenge students to look at their writing for sentences that they can revise. Students can work in pairs to help each other.

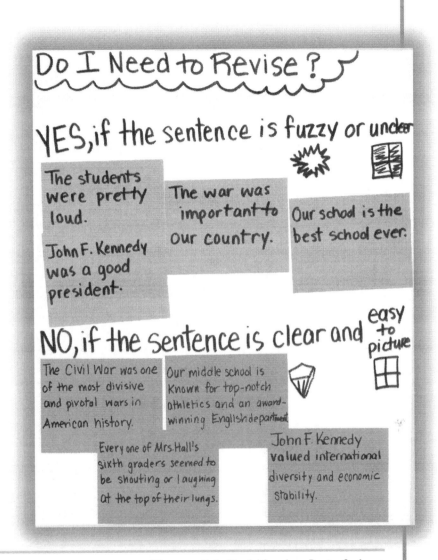

Do I Need to Revise?

YES, if the sentence is fuzzy or unclear

The students were pretty loud.

John F. Kennedy was a good president.

The war was important to our country.

Our school is the best school ever.

NO, if the sentence is clear and easy to picture

The Civil War was one of the most divisive and pivotal wars in American history.

Our middle school is known for top-notch athletics and an award-winning English department.

Every one of Mrs. Hall's sixth graders seemed to be shouting or laughing at the top of their lungs.

John F. Kennedy valued international diversity and economic stability.

Figure 5.1 *Do I Need to Revise?* chart

Elaboration Ideas

If you ask students how to elaborate and add more details to their writing, most students will offer limited responses. They know what you want, but struggle with the strategies to make this happen. This chart was created with seventh graders working on explanatory and argument writing, but is appropriate for all grade levels.

Creating This Chart:

To create this chart, I draw the light bulb in advance. I read a three-sentence paragraph with few details. Then, I ask students how they would stretch this paragraph by elaborating and adding more details. As students share suggestions, I guide them to name a universal strategy that I can add to the light bulb. After they exhaust their ideas, I continue prompting until we add each of the seven strategies.

Teaching Tips:

- After each strategy is added to the chart, write one or two examples on a sentence strip or on a dry-erase board.

- Create this on your wall instead of chart paper. Use each of the strategies as a heading. After teaching each one, ask students to craft and share examples. Add some of these student-generated examples under the name of each strategy.

- Using your science or social studies books, point out sentences that follow these elaboration techniques. If you don't have access to these, consider online articles. You would be surprised how often these techniques show up in the news and in professional writing. Try www.nytimes.com/roomfordebate to get started.

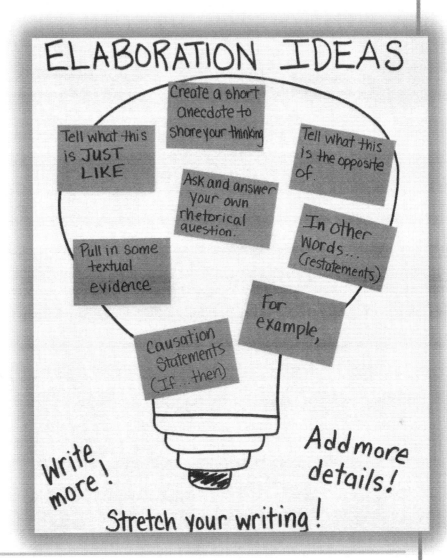

Figure 5.2 *Elaboration Ideas* chart

Rename Your Subject!

While this particular chart was created with a group of third graders, I have created versions of this chart with students as advanced as high school. This chart works for any student who needs tangible ways to avoid restatement of the subject's name unnecessarily within their writing.

Creating This Chart:

The students had read *Charlotte's Web* by E. B. White in class earlier that month. Because of this, I decided to use Charlotte and myself as "pretend" subjects. I wrote both of our names on large sticky notes, then added the chart title. Next, I asked students what pronoun they could use for Charlotte and I instead of our names. When they identified "she" as the correct pronoun, I wrote it down on small, ½"x2" page markers and placed one under each of our names. Next, I asked students to come up with different nouns that could also name Charlotte and I. As they came up with different nouns, I wrote these on different color page markers, adding them underneath our names. After we had at least five, I wrote a sentence about myself, using my name. Then, I asked students to make up a new sentence with a pronoun, followed by another sentence with an adjective and one of the other nouns. On the chart I wrote each sentence, then underlined and named what we did.

Teaching Tips:

- For seventh and eighth graders this standard overlaps with standard four; both standards ask students to think about their audience when revising. This chart is a great opportunity to talk about revision, while keeping audience and purpose in mind. Discuss which types of nouns or combinations might be most appropriate for different audiences.

- Avoid using the names of specific students in your class as subjects for this. It just takes one negative comment to ruin a fun activity like this.

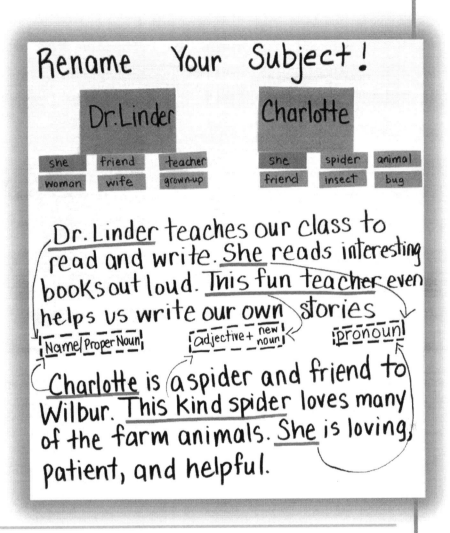

Figure 5.3 *Rename Your Subject!* chart

Revision Lenses

This chart was created with eighth graders who were working on informative essays. Instead of asking the students to revise in general, I asked students to take a look at their work through each of the revision lenses. This resulted in tightly-focused revision.

Introducing This Charts:

I draw this chart from start to finish with students. Typically, I create this in one session with seventh and eighth graders. With students in sixth grade or younger, I like to break this up into small mini-lessons about each of the areas. This would mean introducing *variety* and *audience* together on the first day, but *clarity* and *rhythm* on a separate day. Some teachers even like to introduce one lens and stay focused on that for a week or so, adding additional categories over time.

Teaching Ideas:

- For writers who are reluctant to revise their work, consider asking them to mark their papers with evidence of the revisions. Some teachers have had students circle two sentences that are structured differently or box in the different transitions, etc. to serve as proof that the revision lenses have been used.

- Examine a shared piece of writing and use the questions to revise together.

- For younger writers, consider color-coding each of the lenses. Purchase different color sunglasses from a party or discount store. Allow students to wear the matching color glasses when they are using that revision lens.

- Consider modifying some of the questions to turn this into a checklist. Ask students to answer each question, then find a peer to read their paper and see if they agree.

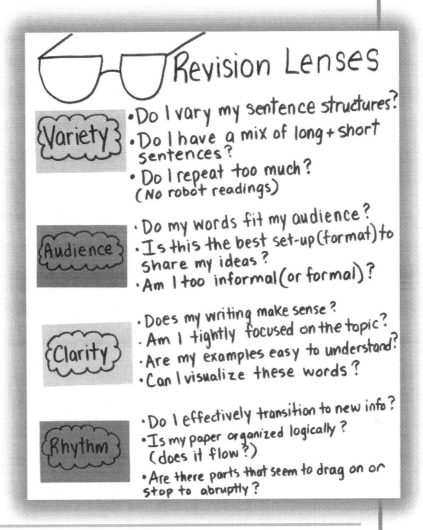

Revision Lenses

Variety
- Do I vary my sentence structures?
- Do I have a mix of long + short sentences?
- Do I repeat too much?
(No robot readings)

Audience
- Do my words fit my audience?
- Is this the best set-up (format) to share my ideas?
- Am I too informal (or formal)?

Clarity
- Does my writing make sense?
- Am I tightly focused on the topic?
- Are my examples easy to understand?
- Can I visualize these words?

Rhythm
- Do I effectively transition to new info?
- Is my paper organized logically? (does it flow?)
- Are there parts that seem to drag on or stop to abruptly?

Figure 5.4 *Revision Lenses* chart

Revision Tasks

I came up with the idea for this chart when I worked with a group of fifth graders who seemed to despise revision! I had tried everything that had been successful before, but to no avail. No matter how many times I asked them to review their writing for places to make their work stronger, they resisted. Most would glance at their work for a few moments, then tell me that they felt good with it just as it was. The key with this chart is that I stopped asking students questions to guide their revisions; I gave them clear directives instead. This way, it became difficult for students to simply nod and tell me that they had revised their work.

Introducing This Chart:

Begin by reviewing some of the writing that your students have been doing. Jot down some common revisions that most of the students could benefit from. These four steps on my chart may not be the same four steps that your students need to take; you might have some other areas of focus. What this chart does is give struggling revisionists a place to begin that is tangible and clear. Introduce each task and provide an example of each. Pair these together on the chart.

Teaching Tips:

1. Connect grammar with this activity. Consider asking students to specifically add descriptive clauses, appositives, or participial phrases.

2. Keep a list of interesting adjectives and verbs in your classroom. Teachers do this a lot with the word *said*, but rarely with verbs and adjectives. Post these on sentence strips around the room to help spark ideas.

3. Avoid just asking students to add in lots of adjectives or adverbs. Those are comfortable, but often do not strengthen writing. Consider this sentence: *The cat ran.* Is *The cat ran quickly* really much better? Precise verbs always win! Compare that to: *The cat darted, The cat flitted,* or *The cat raced.*

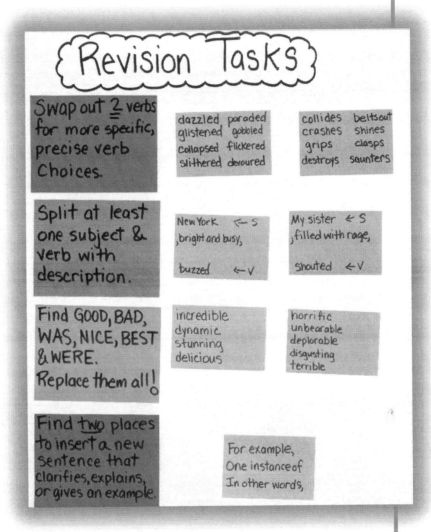

Revision Tasks

Swap out 2 verbs for more specific, precise verb choices.

dazzled paraded
glistened gobbled
collapsed flickered
slithered devoured

collides beltsout
crashes shines
grips clasps
destroys saunters

Split at least one subject & verb with description.

New York ← s
, bright and busy,

buzzed ← v

My sister ← s
, filled with rage,

shouted ← v

Find GOOD, BAD, WAS, NICE, BEST & WERE.
Replace them all!

incredible
dynamic
stunning
delicious

horrific
unbearable
deplorable
disgusting
terrible

Find two places to insert a new sentence that clarifies, explains, or gives an example.

For example,
One instance of
In other words,

Figure 5.5 *Revision Tasks* chart

Say NO! to Lonely Subjects

This chart was created with seventh graders, but can be modified to work with any grade level that understands the basic parts of speech. I find that older students really fall in love with these four ways to revise their sentences. The reason it works so well is because it seems so simple. Students don't have to revise *everything*. With this chart, they can relax a bit and just target the *subject* of the sentence. It is also easy to pick up, so students find success easily and are more open when you explore more ways to revise in the future!

Teaching With This Chart:

I write the title for this chart in advance, but nothing else. I like to add the four types after I explain each one. Some teachers get really creative and draw an octagon-shaped stop sign and write lonely subjects inside the octagon. I begin by telling students that I cannot take reading any more papers with subjects just hanging out all by themselves. Good writers mix it up and give subjects company for variety. I list each strategy, one at a time, discussing each one. Then, I test drive the strategy on a large sticky note.

Teaching Ideas:

1. I like to ask students to try the move out in their notebooks at the same time. Students share what they come up with and offer suggestions and ideas to one another. It becomes a fun time and students enjoy coming up with different ideas.

2. Talk about how audience matters when revising. Name possible audience members and ask students how their word choices might vary. *"How would my language be different if I was revising with the principal in mind? What about my best friend?"* For more audience awareness teaching ideas, see the charts in chapter four.

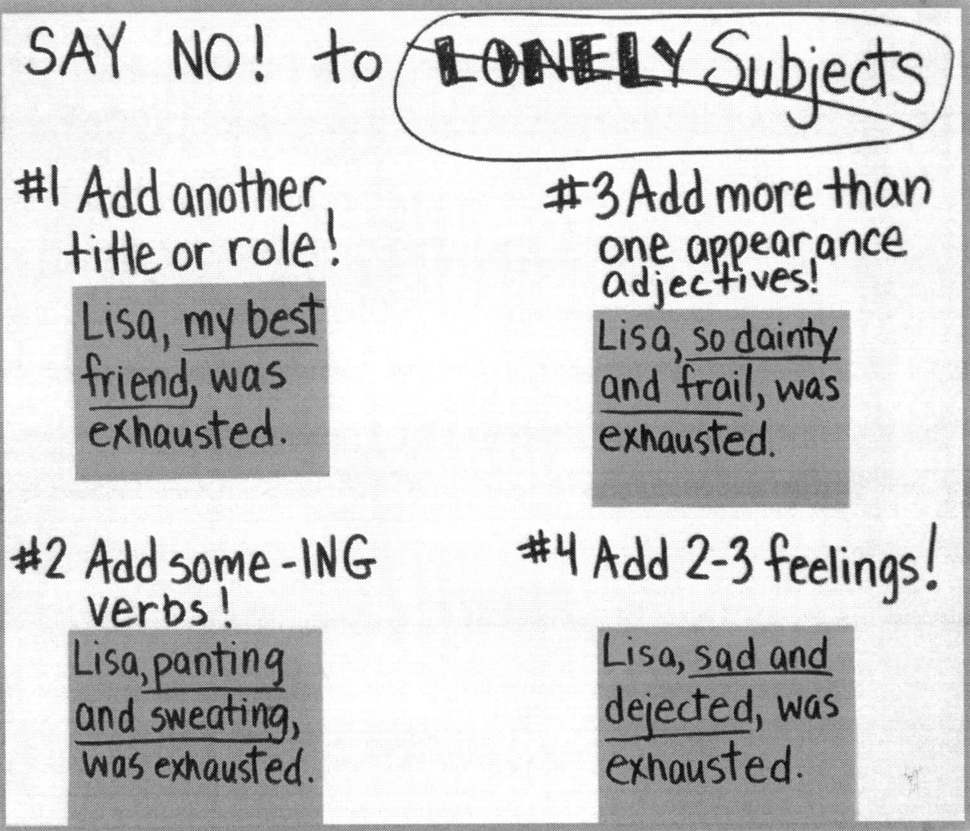

SAY NO! to (LONELY Subjects)

#1 Add another title or role!

> Lisa, <u>my best friend,</u> was exhausted.

#2 Add some -ING verbs!

> Lisa, <u>panting and sweating,</u> was exhausted.

#3 Add more than one appearance adjectives!

> Lisa, <u>so dainty and frail,</u> was exhausted.

#4 Add 2-3 feelings!

> Lisa, <u>sad and dejected,</u> was exhausted.

Figure 5.6 *Say NO! to Lonely Subjects* chart

Use Editing Symbols

I confess: I did not use most of these editing symbols until I was an adult. Somehow I didn't grasp the importance of these as a student. It wasn't until I became a teacher, tasked with helping large numbers of students edit and revise, that I recognized how much my students and I needed a universal language to communicate about changes in our writing. Suddenly, these symbols seemed invaluable for streamlining the editing process.

This simple chart was created with a group of fourth graders at the beginning of the school year. I decided against photocopying a long list of symbols and having students tuck them away in a folder. Instead, I wanted a larger chart that eventually was relocated to an editing center.

Teaching Ideas:

- Some teachers like to write a paragraph on chart paper, filled with the errors that they want to teach the symbols for. Using a different color marker, they add the editing symbols, then place small sticky notes with the name of the editing mark next to the changes. This is a good way to show the editing symbol in action.

- Other teachers have typed a paragraph in need of editing and asked students to share correction ideas. When a student names a correction, that symbol is then added to the chart.

- Once you have introduced the symbols, be sure to use them regularly when you model writing. Let students see you stop, add an editing mark to your writing, and keep going. This is a good way to reinforce that these marks are part of self-editing and can happen at any time in the writing process. They don't have to begin after we have a completed draft. We self-edit constantly.

Figure 5.7 *Use Editing Symbols* chart

Vary Your Sentences

This is one of my favorite charts to create with students. I have made variations of this chart with students in grades second through eleventh. This simple way to add sentence variety is fun and easy to do.

Introducing This Chart:

1. I begin by writing five sentences taken from the introductory paragraphs of argument papers written by the students. For this chart, I used the work from a group of seventh graders.

2. Immediately, students will begin talking and pointing out which sentences they recognize and even announcing if a sentence comes from their work.

3. Next, I explain that there is nothing wrong with any of these sentences, but that I want to show students a way that they can vary these sentences a bit. This is a good time to read any rubric or checklist language that mentions sentence variety or varying sentence structures.

4. At this point, I write the title and tell students that description can precede a subject. I add the first example and we read it together.

5. Next, I call on students to discuss ideas for the subsequent sentences. We share ideas, and continue adding the adjectives.

Avoid Overuse:

Remind students that this is about varying sentence structures. This is not how every sentence should begin, but this is a way to break up repetitive sentence structures and should be sprinkled throughout the paper. I like to compare this strategy to the way we would add sprinkles to an ice cream cone. Too much and you have changed the taste of the ice cream, leaving you with a crunchy mess. Just a sprinkle for flavor, please.

VARY YOUR SENTENCES: Put the Adjectives in Front!

Important, yet easy,
   Recycling helps our planet.

Beautiful and caring,
   My mom is the absolute best.

Invasive and random,
   Locker searches are grossly unfair.

Outdated and sexist,
   Gender-specific sports are a thing of the past.

Inevitable and painful,
   Disappointing events can have a good side, too.

Figure 5.8 *Vary Your Sentences* chart

Writers Share Anecdotes

I struggled with where to place this chart in this book. This could work for multiple standards. I chose to include it with the revision standard because it is one way to elaborate and add more details to writing. Adding more details is a common suggestion that teachers and students tend to offer as a revision suggestion. I have read the work of many students and suggested that a short anecdote might fit well within their work. Unfortunately, this sometimes translates into the idea that they should write a mini-narrative in the middle of otherwise non-narrative writing. To avoid this, I create this chart as a resource for beginning an anecdote within a larger piece of writing. Students select one of the sentence starters and add 2-4 sentences to share the anecdote. This keeps the anecdote focused and to the point.

Grade Level and Genre Considerations:

1. This chart is most appropriate for elementary students who want to add an anecdote to their opinion or explanatory writing. This can either be done under standard five, during revision time, or taught as a type of detail with explanatory or opinion writing.

2. Anecdotes, while an effective strategy, are not as effective with timed-writing middle school argument papers that demand that the author take a third-person look at two sides of a topic. Often this type of writing is expected to reflect a neutral stance, swayed only by facts and data. While debatable, an anecdote may not be as easy to justify as the most effective type of detail to include here.

3. This strategy is not for writing standalone narratives. For more ideas on teaching narrative writing, review chapter three.

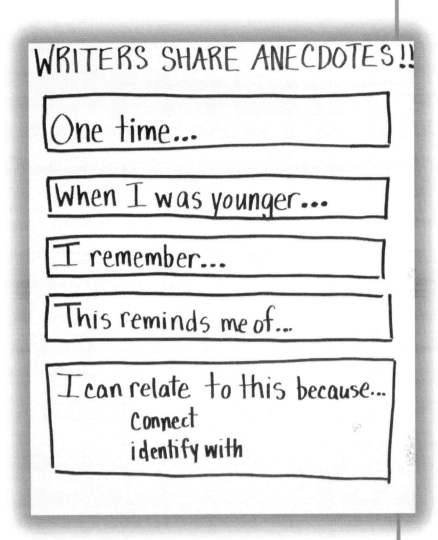

WRITERS SHARE ANECDOTES!!

One time...

When I was younger...

I remember...

This reminds me of...

I can relate to this because...
    Connect
    identify with

Figure 5.9 *Writers Share Anecdotes* chart

Chapter 6

Technology & Writing

Common Core Writing Anchor Standard 6:

Use technology, including the Internet, to produce and publish writing and to interact and collaborate with others.

3 With guidance and support from adults, use technology to produce and publish writing (using keyboarding skills) as well as to interact and collaborate with others.

4 With some guidance and support from adults, use technology, including the Internet, to produce and publish writing as well as to interact and collaborate with others; demonstrate sufficient command of keyboarding skills to type a minimum of one page in a single sitting.

5 With some guidance and support from adults, use technology, including the Internet, to produce and publish writing as well as to interact and collaborate with others; demonstrate sufficient command of keyboarding skills to type a minimum of two pages in a single sitting.

6 Use technology, including the Internet, to produce and publish writing as well as to interact and collaborate with others; demonstrate sufficient command of keyboarding skills to type a minimum of three pages in a single sitting.

7 Use technology, including the Internet, to produce and publish writing and link to and cite sources as well as to interact and collaborate with others, including linking to and citing sources.

8 Use technology, including the Internet, to produce and publish writing and present the relationships between information and ideas efficiently as well as to interact and collaborate with others.

Collaborate with Peers

Standard six focuses on students not only using technology, but being able to write collaboratively. This is very much a function of the mediated, connected culture that our students live in. Meeting the rigor of this standard means stepping outside of "what we have always done." To focus on the collaborative aspect of this standard, I knew that students needed norms for working as a group. This group work could be conducted face-to-face, online, or a combination of both. This chart helps to establish those norms and steps.

Introducing This Chart:

1. I like to introduce this chart near the beginning of the school year. I begin by letting students know that they will work in pairs and/or groups to write and respond to writing several times during this school year.

2. To work effectively, students will need to follow a set of norms so that the work will go smoothly. At this point, I write the chart title and draw the image.

3. I add each checkbox and explain the expectations that I have for collaborative writing.

Collaborative Writing Resources:

- The University of North Alabama offers an alternative way to collaborate using writing roles (similar to literature circle roles): https://www.una.edu/writingcenter/docs/Writing-Resources/Collaborative-Writing-Help.pdf

- The National Writing Project has a wealth of articles filled with ideas for teachingcollaborative writing: http://www.nwp.org/cs/public/print/resource_topic/collaborative_writing

- ReadWriteThink has a great lesson and set of resources to teach collaborative writing: http://www.readwritethink.org/classroom-resources/lesson-plans/collaborating-writing-linking-using-1087.html

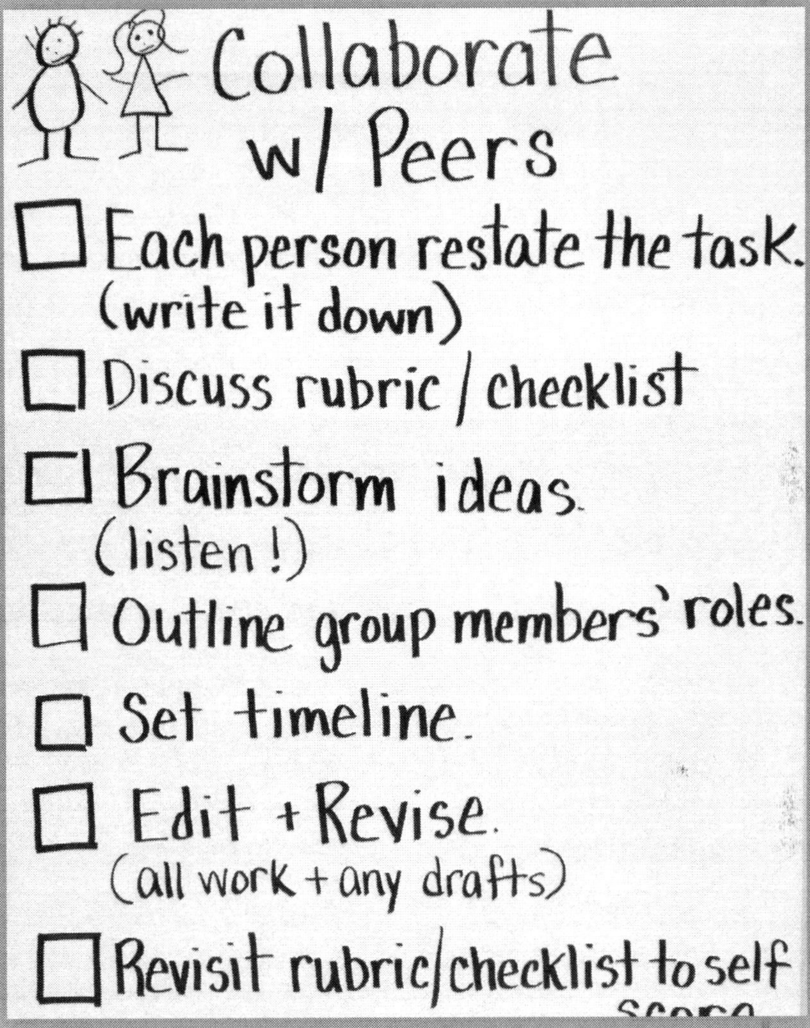

Figure 6.1 *Collaborate With Peers* chart

Digital Writing

Standard six is really the digital writing standard. This is tricky because new digital platforms emerge frequently. What worked last month or year is probably not the most effective strategy a few months or years later. Actively read and stay networked to learn about constantly shifting digital resources and composition tools. If you can get your hands on anything written by Troy Hicks, do it! He has several books on digital writing that are teacher-friendly and resource-rich. Two of my favorites are *Crafting Digital Writing* (Hicks) and *Create, Compose, Connect!* (Hyler and Hicks). You can also find him online at http://hickstro.org.

Introducing This Chart:

1. I begin by adding four types of digital writing on the left side of the chart. I explain what each one is. These four are the ones I felt comfortable introducing. Your list may be longer or vary from mine.

2. Days later, I added *Edmodo* next to *blogs* when the class learned about our new Edmodo class site. Within Edmodo, we created small groups and each group posted a weekly blog, accessible to students and their parents.

3. A few weeks later, we experimented with a class blog on WordPress. At this point, we added *WordPress* to the list.

4. By the end of April, we had the chart that is pictured here. We had experimented with each tool.

Teaching Tips:

- In retrospect, this was a huge challenge to complete with middle school students! If I had a time machine, I would go back and select one tool from each category and spend the year mastering that and that alone.

- Several of the tools here are *not free*. Camtasia® and SnagIt® both cost money. We worked around this by using trial versions, but they were often limited in functionality or expired after 30-60 days. Jing® and Audacity® are both free products.

- If you have a technology teacher at your school, share this standard with that teacher on the first day of preplanning. The learning curve is steep and can be a deal-breaker for those of us who are not digital natives.

Figure 6.2 *Digital Writing* chart

Keyboarding

When I first began teaching in the nineties, I didn't bother much with typing skills. Keyboarding was not my strong point and to be quite honest, I did not feel it was my responsibility to teach. I always viewed this as the role of a technology teacher. I wasn't a technology teacher;- I was a reading and writing teacher. Well, a lot has changed since then! Technology is so pervasive that digital publishing, writing, and online interaction is very much a part of how we communicate. While this cannot be the center of what I teach, it has grown to be a part of what writing is. The standards specifically spell this out for teachers.

Introducing This Chart:

1. I take students to the computer lab or bring in a laptop cart for this lesson.
2. I begin by admitting to students that I am in no way a keyboarding expert, but that being able to type proficiently will help them get more done and make the most of their time.
3. At this point, I draw the picture of the keyboard and add the title.
4. Next, I write the first keyboarding website on the chart and open up the actual site to show students how it works.
5. We continue through each one, asking and answering questions as we go.
6. At this point, I post the chart and allow students to explore the sites on their own for the duration of the class period. I circulate throughout for proximity control and to answer questions.

Ambiguity in the Standards:

According to the standards, fifth graders, for example, should be able to type two pages in one sitting. How long is a sitting? Is a page double-spaced or single-spaced? These are both areas that local schools and teachers have to define for themselves.

KEYBOARDING

Polish Your Skills:

✓ www.typingweb.com

✓ Typing Agent (click the APP icon)

✓ www.bbc.co.uk/guides/z3c6tfr (Dance Mat Typing)

✓ www.abcya.com/keyboard.htm

✓ www.slimekids.com

✓ www.funtotype.com

Figure 6.3 *Keyboarding* chart

Produce/Publish/Collaborate

This chart was created with eighth graders as a resource to illustrate the purposes of different digital tools. Surprisingly, once posted, there were multiple teachers who saw the chart and immediately pulled out a notepad to copy down some of the tools here. The resources here, whether familiar or foreign to you, are constantly evolving. Build your list based on your resources and familiarity.

Creating This Chart:

1. I begin with the title of each category posted on the chart. Then, we discuss how each of the three categories are similar and/or different.

2. Finally, we simply have a discussion about the types of digital tools that writers use to produce, publish, and collaborate. Students always seem to know way more than the teachers do here!

3. This discussion can be twenty minutes or span an entire class period. Adjust it based on the amount of digital resources that you will have access to during the school year, or focus just on the tools that students will be expected to use in the immediate future.

Teaching Tips:

- Don't put anything on this list that you have not already practiced with. Try out the actual task that you want students to use it for. Make the time to play with the technology yourself.

- Collaborate with other teachers to explore some of the less familiar tools together. It only takes a few minutes to set up a Skype® session or register for an Edmodo® classroom.

- Talk to your students about the technology they already use to communicate. Typically, you will learn about new communication tools that you can co-opt for academic purposes.

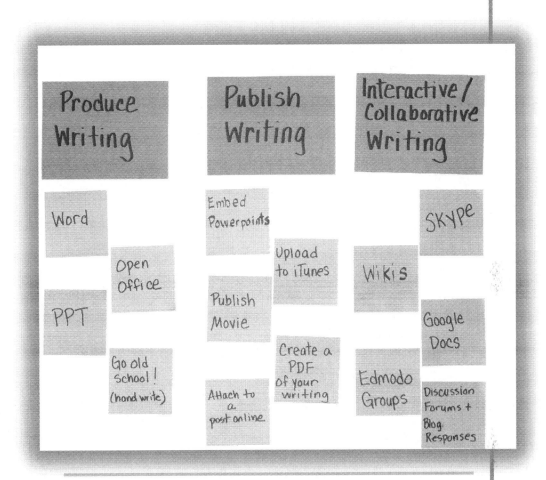

Figure 6.4 *Produce/Publish/Collaborate* chart

Technology and Writing

This chart was created with sixth graders. To align with this standard, composing included multiple phases of drafting, revising, and editing. We outlined the specific tools that the students had access to as they went through the writing process.

Creating This Chart:

1. I write the title in advance, and add the subtitle in front of the students.

2. Next, I ask students to think about the relationship between technology and writing. I like to call on students to share ideas. The real goal is to highlight that technology and writing go hand-in-hand.

3. This is also a great opportunity to discuss different purposes for writing and the importance of audience awareness. Students can explore how different formats might be more effective with different audiences. Standard four focuses on audience awareness. See *Different Audiences* on page 106 for audience awareness teaching ideas.

4. Finally, I write the name of a tool that we have used or discussed before on a sticky note. I ask students when this tool can be useful. After a brief discussion, I add the sticky note next to that category. Notice that some tools are stuck in the middle of two categories. Those are tools that the students felt could work for both categories.

Teaching Tips:

- Consider beginning with only one tool for each area: *planning, composing,* and *publishing.* Require students to use those three tools exclusively. Throughout the year introduce additional digital resources, and require the new format or tool to be used. By the end of the year, you will have a completed list.

- The Microsoft™ (PowerPoint®, Word®, Movie Maker®) and Apple™ (iMovie®) tools are associated with those respective operating systems and are not free. The other resources here can be obtained and used at no cost.

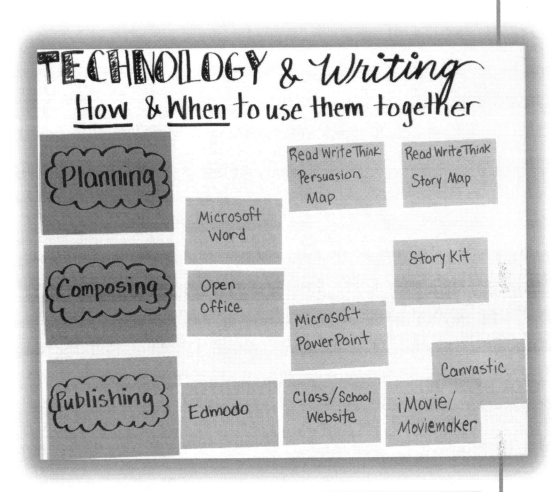

Figure 6.5 *Technology & Writing* chart

Why Do You Need Technology?

Let's face it: most students love technology. The very same assignment you ask a student to complete on paper suddenly becomes so much more interesting if it moves to a digital platform. At times, this results in students asking to go to the computer lab, create a movie, develop a slideshow, or add images to their writing for the sake of interacting with technological tools. The goal for this chart is to set up some guidelines to help students establish why they really need the technology. Technology can be a powerful tool, but should not be used just to check an invisible box that confirms that you use it. Technology use should be purposeful and serve to enhance writing.

Creating This Chart:

1. Typically, I select four or five types of technology that students are already familiar with and/or have had direct instruction with. I list each of the types underneath the title on the left side of the chart.

2. Next, I read each aloud and make sure that the students really do understand what the tools are. When working with younger students, I often have to split this into two lessons; they may be less knowledgeable about some types.

3. Once I am sure that students understand the technology tools, I like to start a discussion about which ones students prefer (or would prefer) to use for their own writing.

4. At this point, I explain, *"Just because we like a digital tool, that doesn't mean we should use it. In class we are working on planning, composing, revising, and publishing to communicate. Let's see if we can figure out valid reasons why these tools make sense for writers."*

5. We did not go in order with our list; we ended up jumping around based on what the students came up with. For continuity, going in order might have made more sense and kept us focused a bit more.

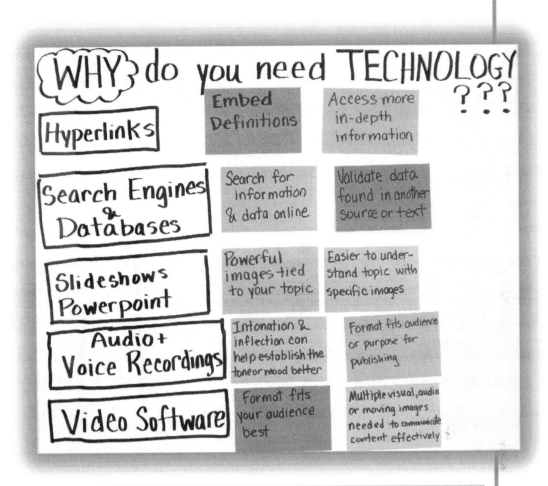

Figure 6.6 *Why Do You Need Technology?* chart

Chapter 7

Research Projects

Common Core Writing Anchor Standard 7:

Conduct short as well as more sustained research projects based on focused questions, demonstrating understanding of the subject under investigation.

3 Conduct short research projects that build knowledge about a topic.

4 Conduct short research projects that build knowledge through investigation of different aspects of a topic.

5 Conduct short research projects that use several sources to build knowledge through investigation of different aspects of a topic.

6 Conduct short research projects to answer a question, drawing on several sources and refocusing the inquiry when appropriate.

7 Conduct short research projects to answer a question, drawing on several sources and generating additional related, focused questions for further research and investigation.

8 Conduct short research projects to answer a question (including a self-generated question), drawing on several sources and generating additional related, focused questions that allow for multiple avenues of exploration.

Animal Research

Standard seven focuses on teaching students how to conduct research. I find that this is a very broad umbrella to teach under. To make it more manageable, I encourage teachers to build this into writing units that are very tightly-focused. For this chart, I worked with third graders who were preparing explanatory reports about different animals. For this age group, beginning research is new and requires lots of scaffolding.

Teaching With This Chart:

1. Students had already selected different animals to research. Most had checked out at least two books about their animals by the time we made this chart.

2. I gathered students on the carpet and wrote the title of the chart. I explained that researching an animal would result in a wide range of information. Good researchers need to have a plan to organize that information effectively.

3. Since I was writing alongside students, I shared that I had already learned where my animal lived. I began describing the animal's habitat. Excitedly, I told them that there was a lot of information about this. I wrote *habitat* on a sticky note and added it to the chart.

4. Next, I asked students to name some other categories of information that they had read about their animals. I wrote these areas on sticky notes and began placing them on the bottom of the chart.

5. After adding the categories, I listed the steps that students would take to organize the information that they found. This gave students a simple way to group their research as they read.

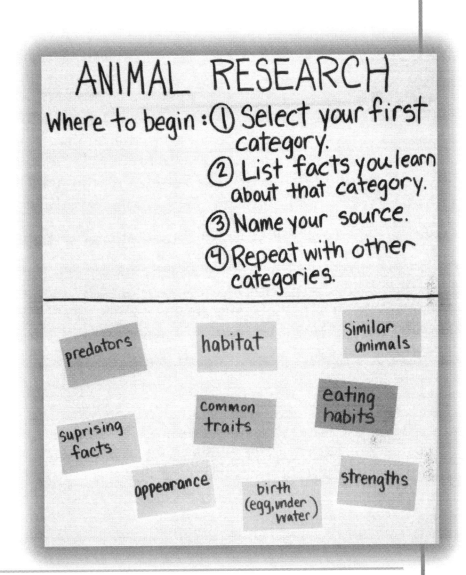

Figure 7.1 *Animal Research* chart

Answering Research Questions

This chart was created with fifth graders who had limited experience researching topics independently. Standard seven specifically states that students should be able to answer questions by relying on multiple sources. I wanted students to have several general resources to consider when beginning their research. When you create a chart like this, consider a wide variety of resources based on what you have access to at your school. This particular class had iPads® and an established Edmodo® classroom.

Introducing This Chart:

For this chart, I made my list in advance, then simply transferred it to the chart in front of the students. I added each checkmark and discussed how to access each tool for research. Please note that I did not include .org sites on the list. Just because a site has this nonprofit extension does not mean that it is actually a nonprofit organization, nor does it mean that the information is reliable. This problem is less likely to occur with .gov and .edu sites.

Interview Resources:

The one category that teachers struggle with including is the *interview experts* suggestion. This section offers resources for possible digital interviews and transcripts that were active at the time of this publication:

- Interviews with artists: http://artfulparent.com/interviews-art-experts-artful-parents
- Interview transcripts about nutrition: http://www.superkidsnutrition.com/nutrition-articles/health-expert-interviews/
- Interviews on multiple topics: http://kids.lovetoknow.com/wiki/Category:Expert_Interviews
- Author interviews (preview first): https://www.goodreads.com/featured_lists/81-ya-author-interviews
- Video interviews with authors: http://www.adlit.org/authors/
- Science experts (students can ask their own questions, too): http://www.allexperts.com/el/Science-Kids/

Answering Research Questions:

✓ Search .gov .edu or school bookmarked sites.

✓ Search scholar.google.com

✓ Check out books on your topic.

✓ Interview experts

✓ Check out apps on the iPad related to your topic.

✓ Ask a question on Edmodo or approved social media sites

✓ Watch a video about your subject.

Figure 7.2 *Answering Research Questions* chart

Different Aspects of a Topic Investigation

This chart was created with a group of eighth graders. We wanted a list of steps that each student could follow and be accountable for as they began their research on different historical time periods. Most students were familiar with research, but they had varying skill levels.

Managing Your Resources:

When I created this chart, I was working with a teacher who taught three different groups of students throughout the day. Aside from the chart titles, we rarely wrote much on chart paper. We always relied on the large 8"x6" sticky notes. This way, we did not waste chart paper making the same chart multiple times. We could still create the charts with students and even vary the charts by putting all of our information on the sticky notes. This allowed for each class to have their own shared experience. If you teach the same content over and over, it is crazy to spend time creating the same chart on different sheets of (expensive) chart paper. What happens to the other two charts when the day is over? If you teach the same subject multiple times throughout the day, try to use the large sticky notes a lot, so that you can still build fresh charts with each class.

Teaching Tips:

1. I used the terms *big* and *skinny* for my questions. These terms refer to broad versus specific questions. The standards don't go into great detail about this; use the terms that work for you.

2. Consider writing on smaller sticky notes. You can arrange these categories in a list. Next to each one, add an illustration to represent that aspect.

3. These are not static aspects. Vary this list to meet the needs of your class and match your research topics.

Different Aspects of a TOPIC INVESTIGATION

Develop both BIG and SKINNY research questions.

Map out more than one set of subtopics for your research.

Investigate and keep track of your sources + experts.

Maintain a good paper trail of your sources & ideas (Word, Zotero)

Be wary of BLOGS + opinion based sources online + in print.

Verify all data, #s, and stats with more than one source.

Figure 7.3 *Different Aspects of a Topic Investigation* chart

Research Categories

This chart is really about moving from broad research questions into very specific research topics. These particular students were at the end of their social studies unit on World War II. Everyone would be writing about World War II, but each person was able to choose which aspect they wanted to research by developing their own research questions.

Preparing for This Chart:

Each box on the left side was written in advance. I told students that we were going to follow these steps in order to develop our research questions and identify possible headings and subheadings for our research. I had spoken with one student in advance (a very bright and brave one) who was willing to volunteer her work for this chart.

Teaching With This Chart:

1. The first thing I did was add the *World War II* sticky note. The students all agreed that this would be the same for everyone.

2. Next, I asked my volunteer to tell the class what big question she wanted to answer. After she shared, I added her question next to the second box. From there, we talked about how to narrow that question even further. Could we make it smaller, more precise, or even narrower? Those ideas went next to the *Skinny ???* box.

3. For the fourth box, we talked about what things we might need to include in order for the reader to make sense of the larger questions. "*What preview information is absolutely necessary?*"

4. Next, we reread her questions and listed the talking points that would make up the core of her paper. These become the *meaty categories.*

5. Finally, we started listing categories that might exist as subheadings. The ones pictured here were just in response to the first *meaty category.* Students had so many ideas that we ran out of room!

6. Students took turns doing this by removing and replacing the sticky notes with their own research questions and ideas.

Figure 7.4 *Research Categories* chart

Steps Researchers Follow

This chart was created with sixth graders to kick off a research unit. Earlier in the year, students had completed multimedia presentations about different authors. Students had been so excited to show their slideshows or movies that they rushed through what really counted. This resulted in lots of poorly-developed projects. This time around, we wanted them to understand that presenting and publishing comes only after a thorough job has been done with the other steps. The title of this chart served to drive that point home.

Creating This Chart:

1. I always draw the feet on the chart in advance (even if it doesn't look like it). I tell students that there are numerous steps that researchers take before they are ready to present their work.

2. Next, I write the text inside of the first foot, explaining what types of questions a researcher thinks about when choosing a topic. I write these questions on small sticky notes and add each above the first foot.

3. After each step, I share an example. For the first footstep, I ask the students if a topic about music would be too broad or too narrow. Then, I ask if "rap music" is too broad or narrow. Students usually agree that a good writer should target a particular aspect of rap, an artist, or a rap event, but that a genre of music is too broad of a topic.

4. We continue through the other steps, following this same pattern of adding the sticky notes and discussing what that step would look like in practice.

5. After the chart is created, students can spend the remainder of the period drafting possible topic ideas. After they come up with two or three possibilities each, they should share their ideas in small groups for feedback.

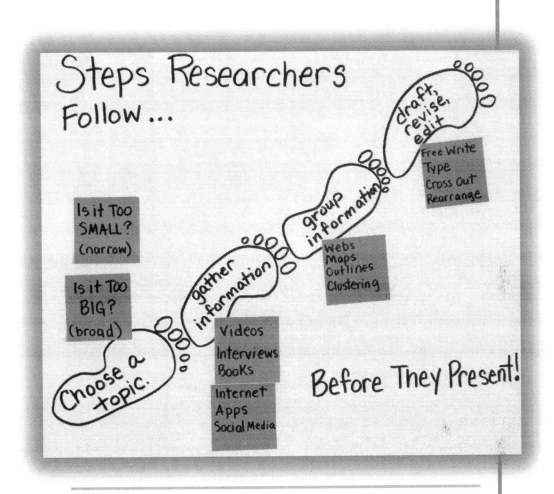

Figure 7.5 *Steps Researchers Follow* chart

Chapter 8

Source Credibility & Plagiarism

Common Core Writing Anchor Standard 8:

Gather relevant information from multiple print and digital sources, assess the credibility and accuracy of each source, and integrate the information while avoiding plagiarism.

3 Recall information from experiences or gather information from print and digital sources; take brief notes on sources and sort evidence into provided categories.

4 Recall relevant information from experiences or gather relevant information from print and digital sources; take notes and categorize information, and provide a list of sources.

5 Recall relevant information from experiences or gather relevant information from print and digital sources; summarize or paraphrase information in notes and finished work, and provide a list of sources.

6 Gather relevant information from multiple print and digital sources; assess the credibility of each source; and quote or paraphrase the data and conclusions of others while avoiding plagiarism and providing basic bibliographic information for sources.

7 Gather relevant information from multiple print and digital sources, using search terms effectively; assess the credibility and accuracy of each source; and quote or paraphrase the data and conclusions of others while avoiding plagiarism and following a standard format for citation.

8 Gather relevant information from multiple print and digital sources, using search terms effectively; assess the credibility and accuracy of each source; and quote or paraphrase the data and conclusions of others while avoiding plagiarism and following a standard format for citation.

Categorize Information

This chart blends the learning from standards seven and eight together. Created with a group of eighth graders, the goal was to help students use their research questions to develop targeted areas of inquiry. These categories could potentially turn into specific headings within their papers, but were really needed to initially organize their informational searches.

Introducing This Chart:

1. I begin by sharing a story about a time when I was researching vacation ideas. *"I was really excited to learn everything I could about Disney cruises. I went online and started looking up cruise information. There was so much information, I instantly got distracted and started looking up random things that I didn't really need to worry about. Guess what? Two hours later I had a bunch of random information, and I just felt confused. I don't want this to happen to you when you start researching your topics."*

2. I ask students to take out their research questions and to think about three big categories that they can focus on to help answer those questions. This way, when they find information, they can organize it easily. *"If something doesn't really relate to a category, then you know you are off-track. This way you won't waste hours and have nothing that you can really use."*

3. Next, I ask for three volunteers to share their research questions. I write the first student's question on a sticky note and add it to the chart next to the *Research Question(s)* label. As a class, we discuss possibilities for the three categories. We repeat this with the other two questions. Extra suggestions are placed at the bottom of the chart.

4. After I created the chart with this group, the students who had not initially volunteered now wanted to add their questions to the chart and have help creating their own categories. This was unexpected! As a result, the three students who originally volunteered served as small group leaders, recreating this activity with the other students.

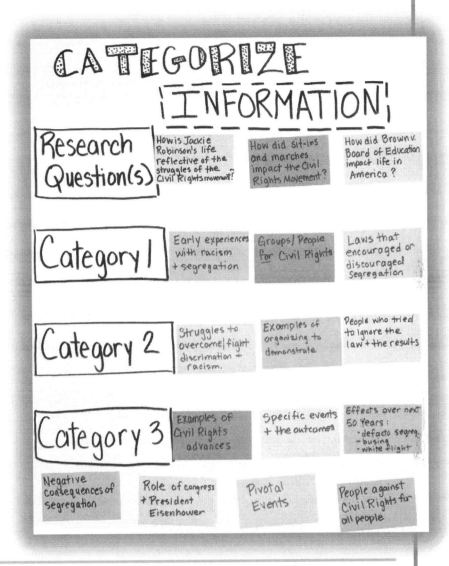

CATEGORIZE
INFORMATION

| Research Question(s) | How is Jackie Robinson's life reflective of the struggles of the Civil Rights movement? | How did sit-ins and marches impact the Civil Rights Movement? | How did Brown v. Board of Education impact life in America? |

| Category 1 | Early experiences with racism + segregation | Groups/People for Civil Rights | Laws that encouraged or discouraged segregation |

| Category 2 | Struggles to overcome/fight discrimination + racism. | Examples of organizing to demonstrate | People who tried to ignore the law + the results |

| Category 3 | Examples of Civil Rights advances | Specific events + the outcomes | Effects over next 50 Years: • de facto segreg. − busing • white flight |

Negative consequences of segregation

Role of congress + President Eisenhower

Pivotal Events

People against Civil Rights for all people

Figure 8.1 *Categorize Information* chart

Gather Relevant Information

When conducting and writing up research, students often end up having information that is redundant, unrelated, or doesn't help to explain their topic. This chart, created with a class of seventh graders, simply provides a set of questions that writers can ask themselves when they are considering whether to include all of the information from their notes or outlines in their drafts.

Creating This Chart:

I draw the thought bubble and title on the chart in advance. I specify that only relevant, credible, and verifiable information should be included in our writing. Then, I begin to write questions that I ask myself to determine relevancy. As I write each question, I add it to the chart. Students will begin making suggestions, too. Generally, the more we talk, the more the list grows.

Variations:

- Instead of using this chart to determine what information should be included in a draft, students can use this as a checklist during the revision process to determine if irrelevant information needs to be deleted or removed.

- These questions are just my suggestions. Develop this list based on more specific information from a rubric or checklist used within your district or one that is included in your writing program.

- Consider drafting short exemplars and non-exemplars. Use the guiding questions to determine if different sentences are relevant or not.

- For the citation question, reference the preferred method of citation (Chicago, APA, MLA, etc.) adopted by your school, as this varies around the country and is not specified in the standards.

Figure 8.2 *Gather Relevant Information* chart

Keep a Log to Recall Information

This chart is specific to the language of the elementary school standards. The standard explains that students should "recall relevant information from experiences." This element of the standard does not exist for middle school students.

Introducing This Chart:

1. I open by asking students to think about their best experience ever, and share with a partner. After a few moments of sharing, I call on a few volunteers to share their experiences with the whole class.

2. Next, I point out that most of the memories that students recalled were from the past few years. "*Why do you think no one shared a memory about being a tiny baby? I didn't hear any crib or learning-to-crawl memories!*"

3. I call on students until we come to the conclusion that most of us don't remember things from that long ago. "*This same thing happens in school. We forget some of our experiences here, too.*"

4. Then, I add the title to the chart and explain that we will use a log to keep track of experiences and learning from now on. As I explain, I draw the rest of the chart.

5. For the last section, I add a few sticky notes to provide students with some ideas for what they might consider for the *My Take* section.

Variations:

- If you teach all subjects, consider creating a science log. Students can keep track of what they learn through lab experiences and science experiments.

- Students can take the logs home to track weekend experiences or other events that might be used to inform other types of writing in the future.

- Modify the style of this log and use this standard to teach students how to take and organize notes.

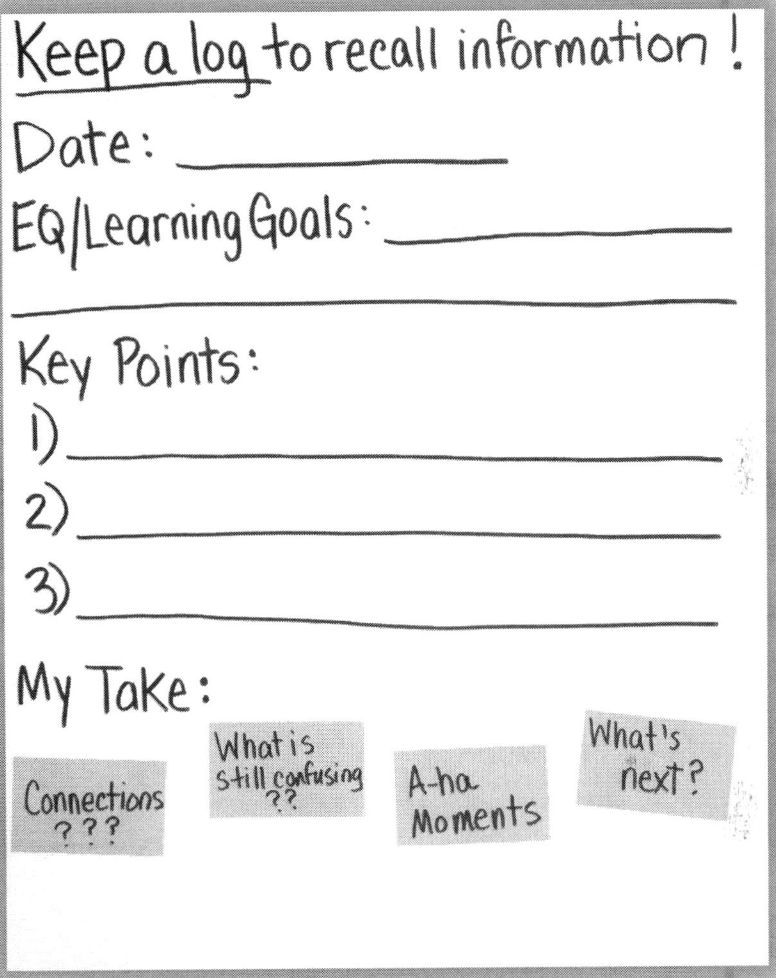

Keep a log to recall information!

Date: _____

EQ/Learning Goals: _____
_____

Key Points:
1) _____
2) _____
3) _____

My Take:

Connections ???

What is still confusing ??

A-ha Moments

What's next?

Figure 8.3 *Keep a Log to Recall Information* chart

Keep Track of Your Sources

I think every single one of us has experienced the terror of losing an important document, misplacing a file, or losing all of our data that we thought had been saved. Whenever I talk with students about the importance of keeping track of their sources, I automatically relive terrifying moments like those.

Teaching With This Chart:

For this chart, I want to not only share some different ways for students to keep up with their source information, but to give them the advantages and disadvantages of different methods. I draw the road and title in front of the students, but I have different cars already drawn on the sticky notes. I stick the cars all over the chart. Each car represents one method. Then, I ask students to talk in small groups about how many of the six ways to track sources they can name. After a few moments, I write their ideas on the car sticky notes. This chart reflects our final list. Always have a few extra cars on standby. You never know if students have a new or interesting method that you had not anticipated.

Tracking Sources:

- Be sure to include methods that match the resources available for your school, but are still well-rounded. I wanted high-tech methods like Zotero® there, but I also wanted to include low-tech options like note cards. The goal is for students to learn about a variety of methods, but stick with what works best for them.

- Zotero® is a free tool to organize and cite sources. A more popular alternative (but not free) is EndNote®. Both have learning curves and are best suited for older students.

- Digital cloud storage services are typically popular among older students. Some students even use their email accounts for cloud storage by emailing updated lists to themselves each time they add new sources. Typing the date and time in the subject line helps students to organize these emails. This is a great way to use email as a cloud-like storage system.

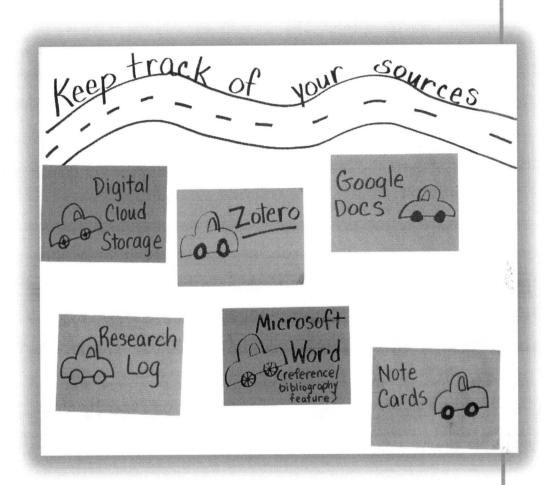

Figure 8.4 *Keep Track of Your Sources* chart

Looking for Credible Sources

This chart is a simple checklist that I created with sixth graders to encourage them to think about the types of sources that they include as references. This chart was specific to these students, based on trends that I saw. For example, Wikipedia was a popular source for students. I had several students that actively argued that this was a viable source. I finally admitted that it was not a horrible choice, but that it could easily be edited anonymously. Our compromise was that students could not cite Wikipedia, but could use the reference list provided on the site to read more, gather information, and possibly list those sources as references, if they met the other criteria.

Creating This Chart:

1. I create the entire chart in front of the students, explaining each criteria individually as I write it on the chart.

2. After each criteria is listed, I like to ask the students for advice about what type of image to draw. I want them to help me create a visual to associate with the criteria. This is always fun to do. Students typically spend time debating what each criteria really means in an effort to prove that their suggested images are best.

3. A day or two later, I like to create smaller bookmarks with these same categories for each student. I usually call these their "Credibility Bookmarks." Students are instructed to have them when they research their topics so that they can check each source against the bookmark before citing the source or adding it to any reference list.

Figure 8.5 *Looking for Credible Sources* chart

Researchers Paraphrase, Cite, and Synthesize!

Intentional (or unintentional) plagiarism is often a problem when it comes to research. Students often copy whole sentences or passages in an attempt to include research in their writing. Teaching students to quote properly can often help with this, but they still face challenges when it comes to paraphrasing and synthesizing information. This chart offers a step-by-step set of instructions to help students put information into their own words and provide a context for that information.

Creating This Chart:

I draw the title and illustrations at the top of the chart, but keep the rest of the chart blank. We spend time discussing the words *paraphrase, cite,* and *synthesize*. After making sure that students understand the terms, I introduce each sticky note and place it on the chart. I just use images for the sticky notes in the center, but I add sentence starters for the other two. I find that students need this scaffold when they are first beginning to cite and explain information gathered from other sources.

Teaching Ideas:

1. Turn this into a list. Have students copy it into their writing folders to refer to throughout the writing process.

2. Expand the sentence starter list by reading news articles. Notice how they cite and attribute information to different sources. Mirror their techniques and add them to your chart as possible sentence starters.

3. For more information on using textual evidence and citations, read chapter one. Argument writing often requires students to paraphrase information. There may be variations or similar charts that align with this same learning. This is common with the writing standards because they overlap and are so interdependent.

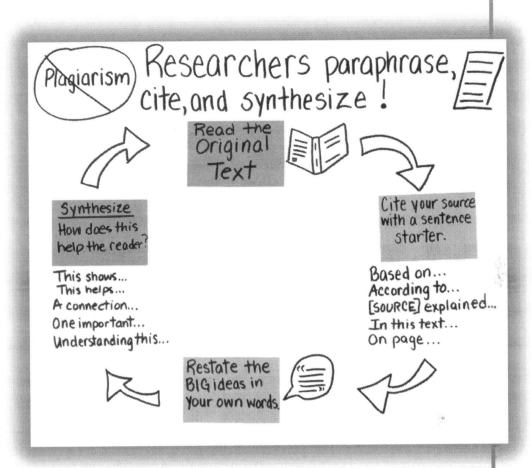

Figure 8.6 *Researchers Paraphrase, Cite, and Synthesize!* chart

Chapter 9

Analyzing Text

Common Core Writing Anchor Standard 9:

Draw evidence from literary or informational texts to support analysis, reflection, and research.

3

(Begins in grade 4)

4

Draw evidence from literary or informational texts to support analysis, reflection, and research.

a) Apply grade 4 Reading standards to literature (e.g., "Describe in depth a character, setting, or event in a story or drama, drawing on specific details in the text [e.g., a character's thoughts, words, or actions]").

b) Apply grade 4 Reading standards to informational texts (e.g., "Explain how an author uses reasons and evidence to support particular points in a text").

5

Draw evidence from literary or informational texts to support analysis, reflection, and research.

a) Apply grade 5 Reading standards to literature (e.g., "Compare and contrast two or more characters, settings, or events in a story or a drama, drawing on specific details in the text [e.g., how characters interact]").

b) Apply grade 5 Reading standards to informational texts (e.g., "Explain how an author uses reasons and evidence to support particular points in a text, identifying which reasons and evidence support which point[s]").

6

Draw evidence from literary or informational texts to support analysis, reflection, and research.

a) Apply grade 6 Reading standards to literature (e.g., "Compare and contrast texts in different forms or genres [e.g., stories and poems; historical novels and fantasy stories] in terms of their approaches to similar themes and topics").

b) Apply grade 6 Reading standards to literary nonfiction (e.g., "Trace and evaluate the argument and specific claims in a text, distinguishing claims that are supported by reasons and evidence from claims that are not").

7

Draw evidence from literary or informational texts to support analysis, reflection, and research.

a) Apply grade 7 Reading standards to literature (e.g., "Compare and contrast a fictional portrayal of a time, place, or character and a historical account of the same period as a means of understanding how authors of fiction use or alter history").

b) Apply grade 7 Reading standards to literary nonfiction (e.g. "Trace and evaluate the argument and specific claims in a text, assessing whether the reasoning is sound and the evidence is relevant and sufficient to support the claims").

8

Draw evidence from literary or informational texts to support analysis, reflection, and research.

a) Apply grade 8 Reading standards to literature (e.g., "Analyze how a modern work of fiction draws on themes, patterns of events, or character types from myths, traditional stories, or religious works such as the Bible, including describing how the material is rendered new").

b) Apply grade 8 Reading standards to literary nonfiction (e.g., "Delineate and evaluate the argument and specific claims in a text, assessing whether the reasoning is sound and the evidence is relevant and sufficient; recognize when irrelevant evidence is introduced").

Modern Stories are Analyze How Influenced

Standard nine is a combination of both the reading and writing standards. Students are expected to write about what they have read to meet the rigor of this standard. This particular chart is specific to the eighth-grade standard, which includes language from reading standard nine, and asks students to analyze how a modern work of fiction draws from themes, events, or character types from traditional, biblical, or mythical stories.

Creating This Chart:

1. I begin by writing the title and asking students how they would plan for this type of analysis. After I hear different ideas and redirect as needed, I tell students that I have a few steps that will help with this type of writing.

2. At this point, I draw each box and name each step as I write it on the chart.

3. I ask students to think of this as the roadmap to follow when they craft their analyses. *"These four steps will help you organize your analysis paper. Each box represents another step."*

4. After naming each step, I return back to the first step and add arrows that list tips about what students should consider when they are working on each area.

Teaching Tips:

- Pair this activity with your introduction of reading standard nine or in a unit directly after introducing the reading standard to your students.

- Select books that clearly draw on traditional stories. Share these titles with students and consider crafting a group paragraph together for one of the steps.

- Pair students in teams to write collaborative analyses. The thinking involved for this type of writing is definitely higher-level; working in teams may be more effective when you introduce this skill.

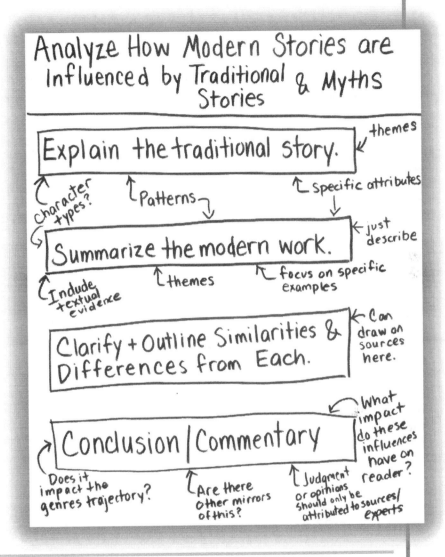

Analyze How Modern Stories are Influenced by Traditional Stories & Myths

Explain the traditional story. ← themes

↖ character types?

↳ Patterns

↳ Specific attributes

Summarize the modern work. ← just describe

↳ Include textual evidence

↳ themes

↳ focus on specific examples

Clarify + Outline Similarities & Differences from Each. ← Can draw on sources here.

Conclusion | Commentary

↰ What impact do these influences have on reader?

↳ Does it impact the genres trajectory?

↳ Are there other mirrors of this?

↳ Judgment or opinions should only be attributed to sources/experts

Figure 9.1 *Alike and Different* chart

Analyzing Literary Devices

A common method of analysis is to read a piece of literature or informational text through the lens of a writer, rather than a reader. This means that students analyze the author's craft. One of the most accessible ways to do this is to examine how different authors use literary devices.

Creating This Chart:

At the beginning of our unit, I created this chart with a group of seventh graders. I added the four large sticky notes to the left side of the chart. Then, I told students that I was going to read a picture book out loud. I wanted them to listen and see if they noticed figurative language, symbolism, or irony in the text. Next, I read Jacqueline Woodson's *This is the Rope* out loud. Then, I asked students what devices they noticed. One of the students suggested that the jump rope was a symbol. As a result, we explored symbolism. As a group, we moved through each of the steps, recording their ideas on the chart. At the conclusion, I told students that we would try this again the next day, but with a grade-level text. See ideas below for next steps based on the grade that you teach.

Teaching Tips:

- This standard is not applicable to third graders; it does not begin until the fourth grade.

- For fourth and fifth graders, I suggest targeting one or two specific devices and reading another picture book out loud. Repeat the experience from the day before. The next day, try it again by reading a book out loud, but have students work in small groups or pairs to analyze it.

- For sixth graders, consider expanding the list of devices up to four. I would still consider a shared text at this point, but would move to a grade-level appropriate text.

- For proficient writers with a strong understanding of literary devices, let them select a text of their choice and do not specify which devices they must write about. Allow students to explore and choose what they highlight.

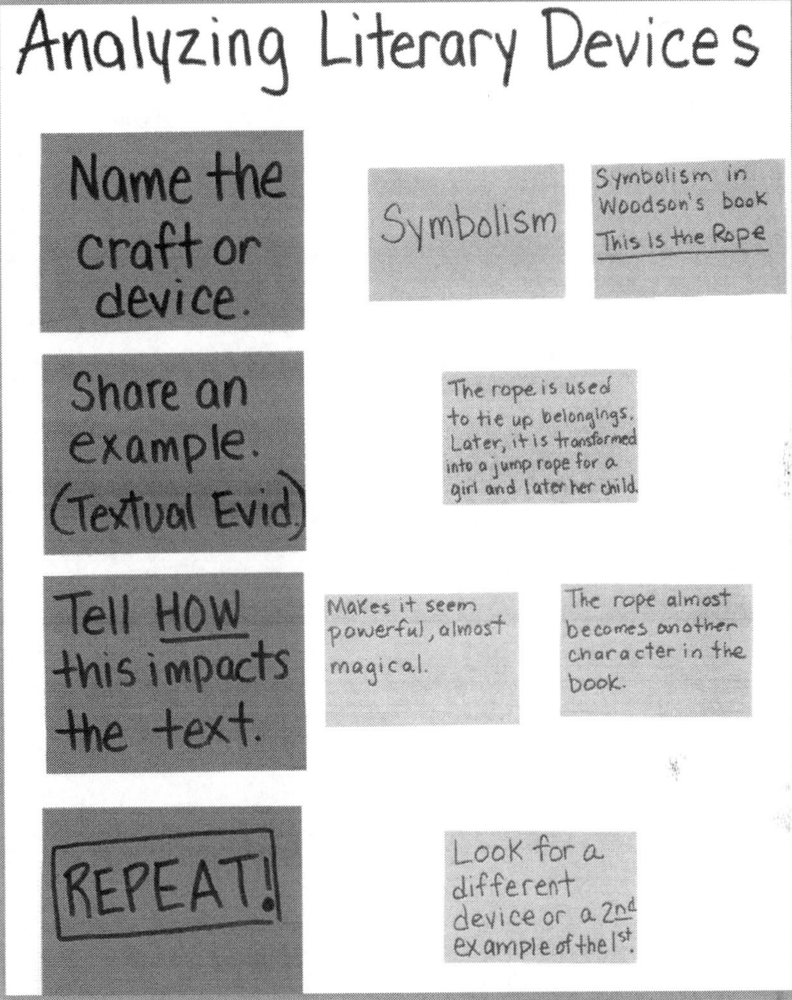

Analyzing Literary Devices

Name the craft or device.

Symbolism

Symbolism in Woodson's book *This is the Rope*

Share an example. (Textual Evid.)

The rope is used to tie up belongings. Later, it is transformed into a jump rope for a girl and later her child.

Tell HOW this impacts the text.

Makes it seem powerful, almost magical.

The rope almost becomes another character in the book.

REPEAT!

Look for a different device or a 2nd example of the 1st.

Figure 9.2 *Analyzing Literary Devices* chart

Be a S.T.A.R.

At first glance, this standard seems to be just about literature, but it isn't. Read closely and notice that the language of the standard slants toward analyzing how authors craft arguments and support their points through reasons and evidence.

Introducing This chart:

1. For this chart I usually pull up a short article from *The New York Times'* *The Learning Network* (http://learning.blogs.nytimes.com) or Roger Ebert's movie reviews (http://www.rogerebert.com/reviews).

2. I select a piece to project on the screen, then we read it together. I try to discuss the piece as much as time allows. It is always a great idea to think aloud and interact with your writers here.

3. Next, I write the title on the chart and tell students that we all want to be STARs. *"STARs examine how authors use reasons and evidence to support their points."*

4. We begin by stating one of the author's claims. You can do this for one major point in the text, or the larger argument for the entire piece.

5. Follow each letter of STAR and write a few sentences to address each one. In the end, you will have written one shared paragraph.

6. Project a new piece of writing on the board and read it out loud. Ask students to create a STAR analysis independently or in pairs.

7. Each time you do this, move on to a longer, more rigorous text.

Teaching Tip:

This is also a great chart to use when teaching standard two. Both standards focus on recognizing or developing strong reasons and evidence to support ideas.

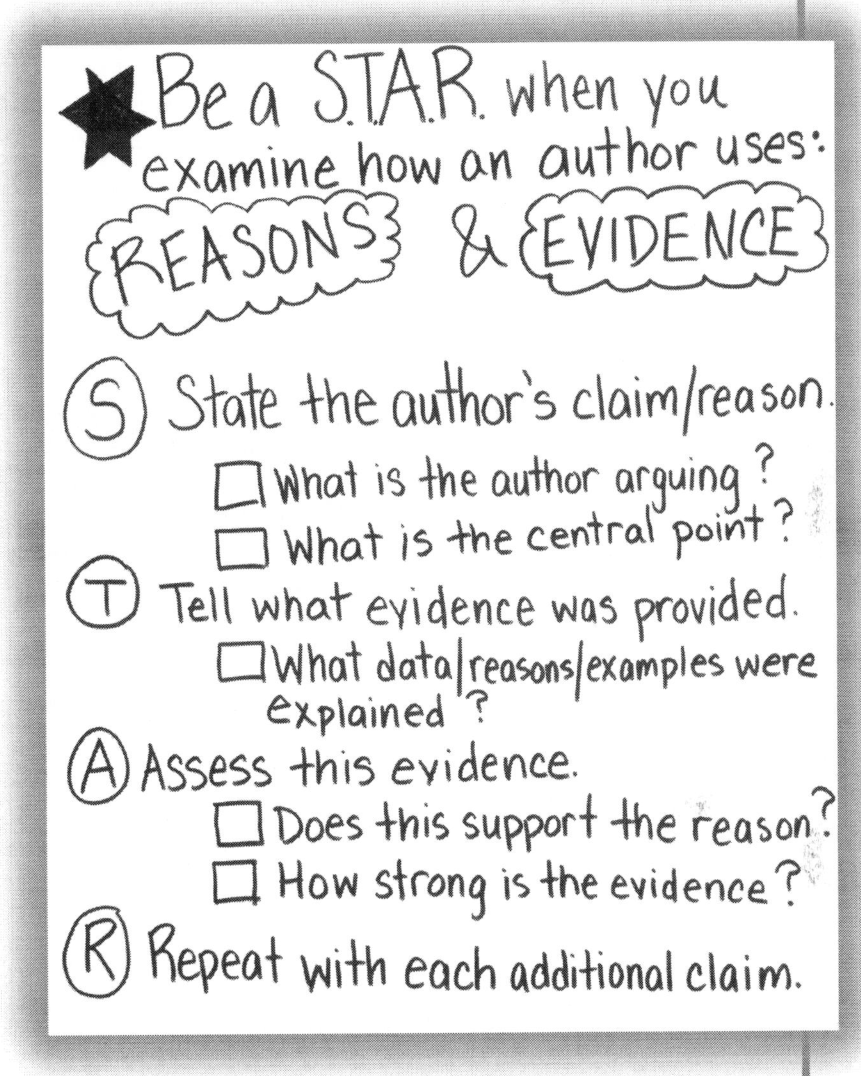

★ Be a S.T.A.R. when you examine how an author uses:
REASONS & EVIDENCE

(S) State the author's claim/reason.
☐ What is the author arguing?
☐ What is the central point?

(T) Tell what evidence was provided.
☐ What data/reasons/examples were explained?

(A) Assess this evidence.
☐ Does this support the reason?
☐ How strong is the evidence?

(R) Repeat with each additional claim.

Figure 9.3 *Be a S.T.A.R.* chart

Recipe for a Literary Analysis

This chart was created to help students form topic sentences for their literary analysis essays, but could be modified to work with informational text as well. The fourth graders (the first grade that has this standard) that worked on this chart had never written to analyze literature. Most of their writing about books had been in the form of book reviews or summaries.

Introducing This Chart:

1. I begin by telling students that a literary analysis topic sentence announces what you plan to say about a book. With older students, I transition to the word *thesis*. You may consider doing that with fourth graders as well.

2. Next, I tell students that they all need one topic sentence, but that this sentence will contain three different parts.

3. I list the parts on the chart and describe each step. I spend a lot of time on step two. I want students to recognize the different verbs and understand what each one means. Other verbs to consider: *explores, explains, depicts, challenges,* or *reflects.*

4. Next, I create the sentence shown here, writing each part on a different sticky note as I add it to the chart. Then, I put students in pairs and ask them to come up with their own literary analysis sentences for the same book.

5. After ten minutes of talking and writing, I have students come back together and share ideas, taking turns replacing my *Maniac Magee* example with their own ideas. We spend the rest of the period experimenting with this.

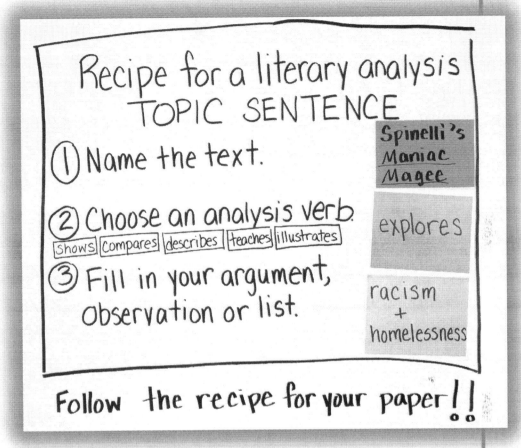

Recipe for a literary analysis TOPIC SENTENCE

① Name the text. — Spinelli's Maniac Magee

② Choose an analysis verb. — explores
[Shows] [Compares] [describes] [teaches] [illustrates]

③ Fill in your argument, observation or list. — racism + homelessness

Follow the recipe for your paper!!

Figure 9.4 *Recipe for a Literary Analysis Topic Sentence* chart

Target a Focus for Your Literary Analysis

This chart was created with eighth graders during the culmination of a unit on literary analysis. Students had written two guided analyses where they were told to write about very specific aspects of two different books. For their final analyses, they were able to select their own books. This chart was there to guide them toward rich ideas and concepts to explore in hopes of avoiding simple character descriptions or book reports.

Teaching Ideas:

1. To create this chart, I prepare everything in advance. I use this shape because I want students to think about targeting or narrowly focusing their writing.

2. I place the individual sticky notes on random desks in the classroom before the students arrive.

3. When the students enter the class, everyone with a sticky note can stand on one side of the classroom and hold their sticky note in front of them as they read it out loud.

4. The other half of the class is told to silently partner with another student who is holding a sticky note that they find interesting.

5. Once students split into pairs, they discuss what the notes mean. From there, we simply have a conversation about each topic.

6. After we discuss a topic, I like to summarize the discussion, then add it to the bullseye. Students are asked to record a few ideas from the chart that interest them and the names of three or four books that they are considering.

7. The next day, we typically spend time revisiting the list and brainstorming possible areas of focus for their final projects.

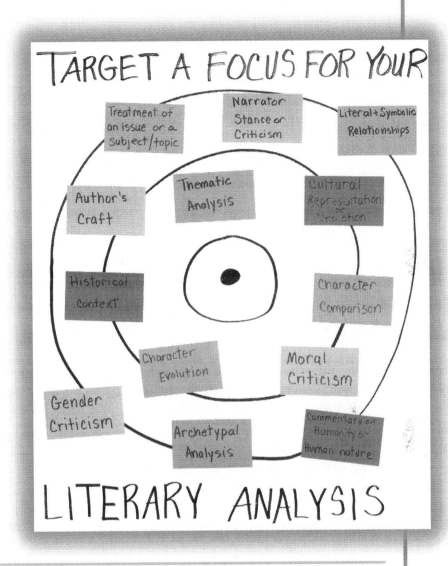

TARGET A FOCUS FOR YOUR

- Treatment of an issue or a subject/topic
- Narrator Stance or Criticism
- Literal + Symbolic Relationships
- Author's Craft
- Thematic Analysis
- Cultural Representation or Depiction
- Historical Context
- Character Comparison
- Character Evolution
- Moral Criticism
- Gender Criticism
- Archetypal Analysis
- Commentary on Humanity or Human nature

LITERARY ANALYSIS

Figure 9.5 *Target a Focus for Your Literary Analysis* chart

Organizing Your Literary Analysis

Literary Analysis. For elementary and middle school students, this can be a scary term. I love to make this chart to help students see that organizing this type of writing is simple, if broken into bite-sized pieces.

Teaching With This Chart:

1. To get started, I gather several different picture books. I try to select books that have an obvious symbol, theme, archetype, or historical setting. I read excerpts from each book out loud. You won't need to read the entire book, just enough so that you can reference the theme, archetype, symbol, or historical setting in the book. Read in advance to mark the pages you want to read.

2. After reading out loud, I begin to create the chart. I add the title and the large sticky note that reads: *Identify your literary focus,* followed by each of the sticky notes from that column to the chart.

3. Next, I ask students to talk about which area they could focus on if they were writing about *Rosa* by Nikki Giovanni (students will have multiple, varied ideas—that's good). We repeat this for each book.

4. I explain that the next step is to find examples in the book to prove the theme or archetype that has been identified. At this point, I place all of the sticky notes from the middle column on the chart. I call on students to share examples from each book.

5. Finally, I complete the last column by adding and discussing each sentence starter.

Picture Books to Consider:

- *Red Kite, Blue Kite* by Ji-Ji Jiang
- *Rosa* by Nikki Giovanni
- *Stand Tall, Molly Lou Melon* by Patty Lovell
- *Thank you, Mr. Falker* by Patricia Polacco
- *The Rope* by Jacqueline Woodson
- *Those Shoes* by Maribeth Boelts
- Any version of *Cinderella* or *Snow White*

Organizing Your Literary Analysis

Identify your literary focus	Select at least three examples or instances that illustrate this <u>focus.</u>	• Describe the example. • Tell how it reflects this focus. • Clarify or expand on this connection.
Themes	comparisons or Characteristics	This shows... explains... illustrates...
Archetypes	specific story or character traits	This reflects... supports... is similar...
Symbolism	multiple objects or events in the text	In other words...
Historical (In) Accuracy	different "times" in the text	This means...

Figure 9.6 *Organizing Your Literary Analysis* chart

Notes

Chart Ideas

Final Thoughts . . .

Whether you are a novice or a veteran teacher, I hope that *Chart Sense™ for Writing* has ignited a passion for using visual aids to teach writing. Visual aids, when created with your students, are meaningful and resonate with writers. Being an artist or creating the most colorful and attractive chart is never the focus. The goal is to create mental images that help students become better writers. Obviously, you wouldn't need (or want) to create every chart in this book, but I hope that these examples inspire you and spark lots of teaching ideas! Creating charts with your students not only strengthens your writing instruction, but builds a strong sense of community and shared learning in your classroom.

Ready to continue the conversation? Have questions? Visit me online at **www.rozlinder.com** for teaching ideas.

Happy reading and writing!

Dr. Roz

About the Author

Rozlyn Linder, Ph.D. is a dynamic and highly sought-after presenter, literacy consultant, and best-selling author. Known for her energetic, fast-paced seminars and workshops, she has traveled throughout the United States modeling literacy best practices, leading professional development, and working with schools to improve their writing and reading instruction. An award-winning teacher, she has taught at all levels from elementary through college. She is passionate about motivating students through explicit instruction and the development of standards-based classrooms. Rozlyn and her husband, Chris, have two spirited daughters who love to read and write.